BARGELLO
STITCH

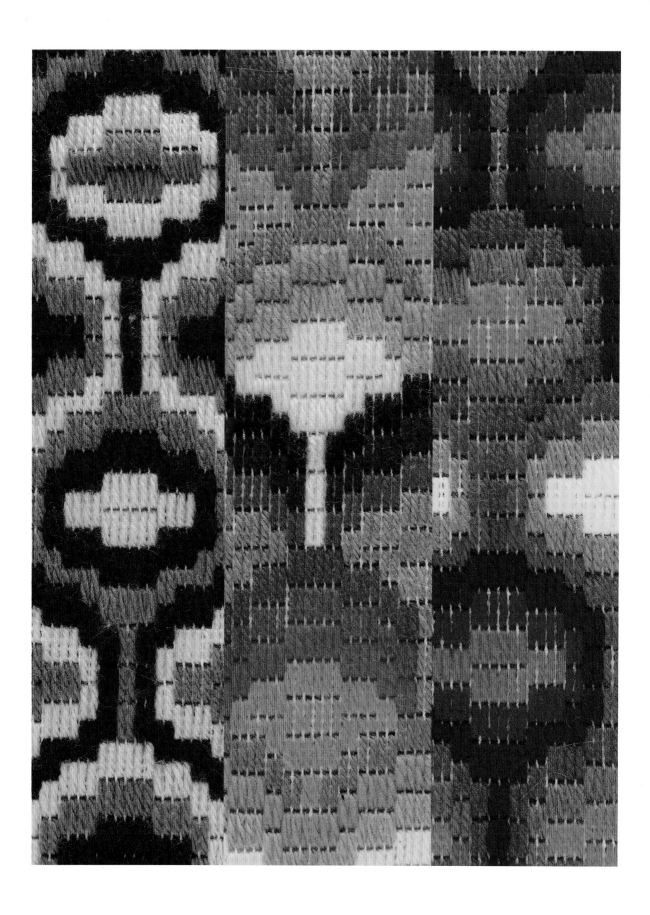

BARGELLO
STITCH

A PATTERN DIRECTORY
FOR DRAMATIC NEEDLEPOINT

LAURA ANGELL AND LYNSEY ANGELL

Search Press

A QUARTO BOOK

Copyright © 2020 Quarto Publishing plc.

This edition published in 2020 by
Search Press Ltd
Wellwood
North Farm Rd
Tunbridge Wells
Kent TN2 3DR

ISBN-13: 978-1-78221-867-8

QUAR.329770

Conceived, edited and designed by Quarto Publishing plc.
6 Blundell Street, London N7 9BH

Senior Editor: Ruth Patrick
Deputy Art Director: Martina Calvio
Designer: Jacqueline Palmer
Editorial Assistant: Charlene Fernandes
Photography: Phil Wilkins
Illustrator: Kuo Kang Chen
Publisher: Samatha Warrington

Printed in Singapore by COS Printers

2 4 6 8 10 9 7 5 3 1

CONTENTS

MEET THE
BARGELLO SISTERS

Laura Angell is a contemporary artist based in the West of Ireland. I have shown work both nationally and internationally. My work is in both government and private collections. I studied fashion and fine art, both of which inform my work.

I am always on the lookout for old techniques and crafting practices to reinvent and evolve with my own twist. I stumbled across bargello while researching new ideas and techniques. Although there was little information available, I started working from a handful of images that I sourced on the internet. The reason I wanted to write this book is to provide the resource that I searched for, but couldn't find, when I started out on my bargello journey.

Once you've learned the basics of bargello, you can add your own ideas. Nothing is set in stone; mix things up and play around with colour and texture. Bargello is also for fun and relaxation; I find the making process just as rewarding as the final result, if not more.

Lynsey Angell likes making, building and fixing things.
I am a crafter, maker and writer based in the north of England. I work as an artist assistant and also make my own projects. My passion for bargello has grown from a childhood practising cross-stitch samplers to wanting to create and share my designs and colour ideas.

Laura and Lynsey work together as **The Bargello Sisters**.

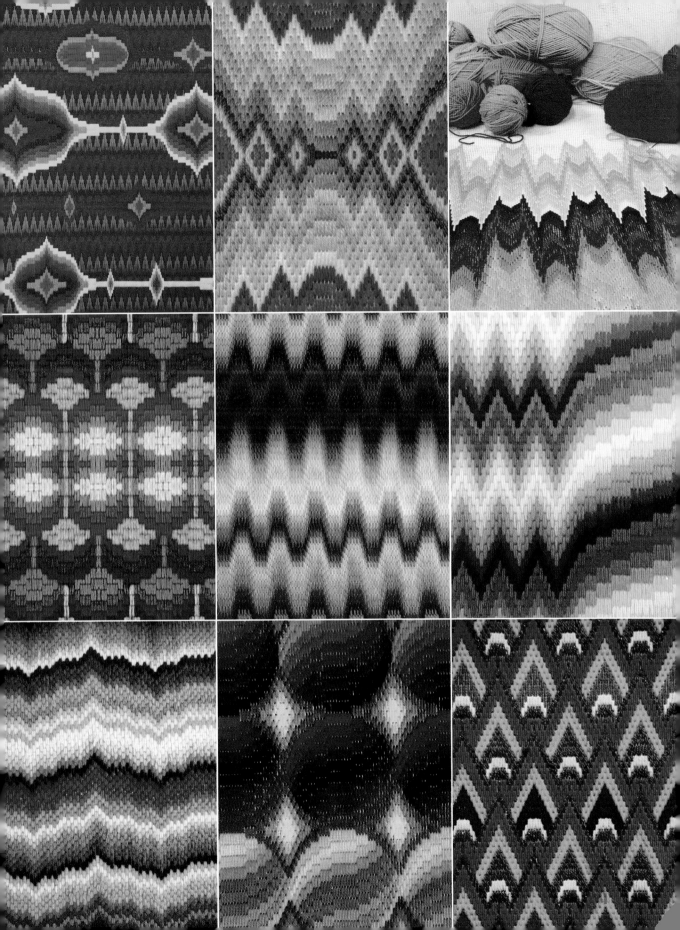

INTRODUCTION

Bargello work is mysterious in origin. There are numerous theories, but no definite history has been documented. Also known as Florentine embroidery, flame stitch, long stitch and Hungarian point, the accepted legend is the most romantic: that the style was brought to Italy when a Medici nobleman married his Hungarian bride in the fifteenth century. Early examples of chair coverings can be found in the Bargello Museum in Florence, but there is no historical information on the method of the craft.

The bargello stitches are counted, distinctive repeated patterns. This type of needlepoint is worked on mono canvas with vertical stitches, usually in wools. Tapestry yarns have long been the expected medium; however, many other yarns and threads can be brought to this toolbox for texture, variety and economy. Our mission is to bring bargello work into the twenty-first century, respecting its medieval origins, while also incorporating the colours of Art Deco, Americana, rococo and the 1970s.

Traditionally, the technique relies for much of its effect on the shading of the colours, most often fading in bands of similar tones. We strongly encourage this when learning the basic technique, but then equally urge you to rip up that rule and use colours you think look great together – be they complementary colours, metallics or mixed textile yarns. The joy of bargello comes from celebrating the colours as much as the patterns.

The patterns fall into two main categories: those worked across the canvas in curved or zigzag rows and motif or medallion designs. In both cases, the stitches are the same length, with the exception of Hungarian point designs, which consist of rows of short stitches interspersed with long ones.

Bargello embroidery is suitable for both decorative panels and larger wall hangings, a number of domestic items such as cushions and chair seats, and accessories such as bags and belts. We have also used it to refresh upholstery or to darn a favourite clothing item with style.

As a discipline, bargello work is known to have great mental health benefits, due to its rhythmic counting quality and joyful use of colour, as well as the satisfaction gained from making something beautiful. Taking up bargello as a hobby is inexpensive, and the tools and materials are easy to source. We began this journey with little more than a single tapestry needle, a few leftover balls of yarn and a pencil and ruler. We haven't needed much else, although we have to 'fess up that our wool collections have grown immeasurably since!

TOOLS AND MATERIALS

Beginning your bargello journey is inexpensive and easy. The equipment is largely unchanged from its early days and can be found in haberdashery shops, most department stores and on the internet.

The basic kit is a tapestry needle, a mono canvas, a pencil and ruler, scissors and some yarns. When using mono or duo canvas (not plastic) many needlepointers prefer a hoop to hold and to focus the work. A thimble is also optional, depending on how you prefer to sew. Later on, in order to present your work, you will use finishing techniques to block the work with a steam iron (see page 13) and a staple gun for mounting onto a solid frame (see page 24).

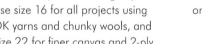

NEEDLES
A tapestry needle is distinctive due to its blunt point and large eye. We use size 16 for all projects using DK yarns and chunky wools, and size 22 for finer canvas and 2-ply or metallic threads.

THIMBLE
A thimble is not only used to protect your hands from rough weft and the needle, but also the fabric from dirty fingers. Not all needlepointers use thimbles and it will very much depend on how you prefer to work.

RULER
This is an essential piece of kit. When practising bargello you cannot check your lines often enough: 'Check now and save lengthy unpicks later' is our motto! We prefer a clear 30cm (12in) ruler so that you can see your stitching through it and count accurately.

PENCIL
When planning your work, it is useful to mark out the centre of your canvas and sometimes divide it into sections, depending on the complexity of the design. A pencil is preferable to pen as it won't show through your work and can also be erased.

SCISSORS
A small pair of well-kept scissors is essential as you are going to be cutting a lot of lengths of yarn. A pair with blades of up to 5cm (2in) is ideal; however, for cutting canvas you will require longer blades, up to 10cm (4in).

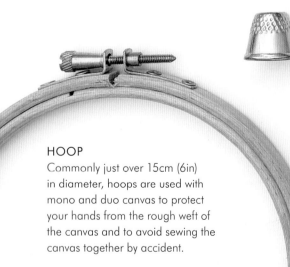

HOOP
Commonly just over 15cm (6in) in diameter, hoops are used with mono and duo canvas to protect your hands from the rough weft of the canvas and to avoid sewing the canvas together by accident.

YARNS

Choosing yarns is undoubtedly the most enjoyable part of project planning. Our rule of thumb is that if you can thread it into a needle, you can sew with it.

Many needlepointers prefer to use only tapestry wool, as it sits nicely and maintains a uniform finish; however, ranges of tapestry wools tend to have limited colour choices and can be expensive to use, particularly on larger pieces.

We rip up the rule book completely on this. The diversity of yarn colours and textures out there is so vast and so inviting that we want to use it all. Bringing new textures and tones to bargello has completely refreshed the art for us and we will show you how to do this, too.

DK ACRYLICS AND COTTONS
This is standard 8-ply hand-knitting wool. Acrylics have the largest range of colours and are strong enough to enable you to use long lengths – up to approximately 90cm (3ft) – without stretching. With cottons, use shorter lengths of about half the size as this material can tangle easily.

MACHINE YARN
This is normally 2 ply and 4 ply, and comes in cones. You can use machine yarn on smaller-gauge mono canvas (14CT and up), or simply double it up on the needle and use as a DK.

METALLIC THREADS AND LUREX YARNS
Use these in the same way as 2- and 4-ply yarns, because there's nothing like putting a bit of sparkle in your projects!

SUPER CHUNKY
Available in wools and acrylics, super chunky can only be used on 10CT canvas and larger. It sits particularly nicely on plastic canvas and covers well.

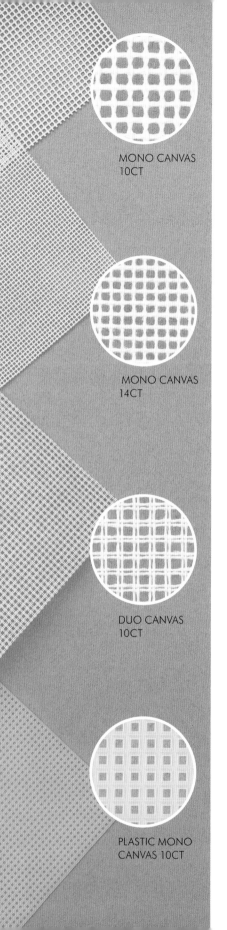

MONO CANVAS
10CT

MONO CANVAS
14CT

DUO CANVAS
10CT

PLASTIC MONO
CANVAS 10CT

CANVAS

To achieve consistent bargello, it is very important to count the threads – for this reason, Mono canvas 10CT has been used for the samples in this book. Canvas choice will vary according to the type of project, so here we have covered the main canvas types to use when you are trying out the featured designs for your own projects.

MONO CANVAS 10CT
This is a real all-rounder that is stiff to handle and doesn't warp easily. For wall hangings, decorative panels and most general uses, its versatility extends to holding almost all yarns.

MONO CANVAS 14CT
The difference between this and the 10CT goes further than the smaller meshes. The scope to use finer stitches and threads opens up the prospect of smaller projects such as handbags, wallets and evening bags.

DUO CANVAS 10CT
As the name suggests, this canvas uses a double thread to make up the meshes. Less stiff than mono canvas, it is best suited to upholstery and soft furnishings. Suits most yarns.

PLASTIC MONO CANVAS 10CT
These are rigid boards, excellent for beginners to practise on, and widely available in many sizes. Used for structural projects such as placemats, decorative boxes, larger bags and even earrings.

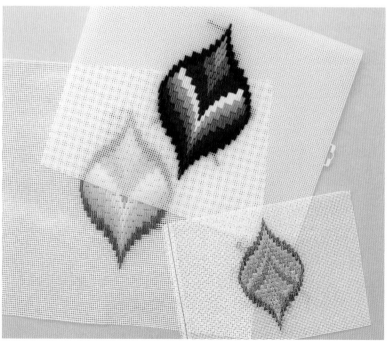

Pomegranates worked on various canvases (see opposite).

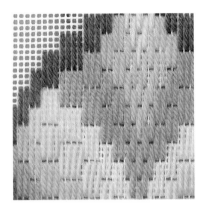

POMEGRANATE ON MONO CANVAS 10CT

This Pomegranate is made using a range of acrylic DK yarns in complementary teal shades, all sourced from local habadashery shops. This will also transfer to cotton DK or natural wools.

POMEGRANATE ON MONO CANVAS 14CT

Made only with metallic thread (from polyester/viscose), this Pomegranate highlights the delicacy that can be achieved using a finer canvas and threads. You could also use 2- and 4-ply machine yarns or lurex yarns.

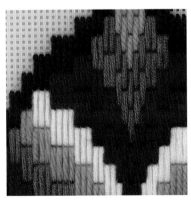

POMEGRANATE ON PLASTIC MONO CANVAS

The robustness of this material lends itself to the use of these fabulous, super chunky acrylic and cotton yarns. Arans, bouclés and multi-thread yarns will also work, but thinner yarns can get lost on this mesh.

BLOCKING

Blocking techniques are used to even out the tension and set, and give a professional finish to your work. You will need a steam iron and a pair of towels. Place the work between the towels and set your iron to a medium/high setting. Using the steam setting, gently press the work until it is crisp and flat. Be particularly careful with metallic threads that you don't have the iron too hot or they could melt!

CHAPTER 1

THE STITCHES

Do you have your tapestry needle and mono canvas ready? It's time to learn some bargello stitches to guide you on your journey. We will show you every stitch used in this book, to equip you to confidently tackle any and all of the designs. From basic brick stitches through curved stitches and to some of the more complex filler stitches, it's all here.

CLIMBING BRICK STITCH

The climbing brick stitch, also known as Gobelin filling stitch, is a bargello basic. Easy to master, it forms the basis of the curve, flame and Hungarian stitches. It can be used to form bands and borders, and to fill in background areas.

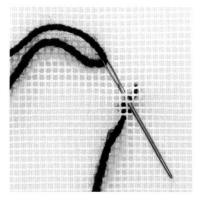

1 Thread the needle, make a knot and pull through the mono canvas. From your first point of entry, count up vertically, leaving 3 meshes, and exit at the 5th mesh. Enter the needle in the next column, 3 meshes down from your exit point. This will be adjacent to the centre of the first part. Pull the thread.

2 Move up again past 3 meshes and exit at the 5th mesh. Enter again in the next column 3 meshes down and adjacent to the centre of the last stitch. Pull the thread through.

3 Repeat step 2. You should start to see a uniform climbing stitch forming by this point.

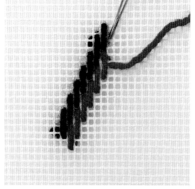

4 Continue to repeat step 2 for the required number of stitches. You can repeat the row underneath in the same or another colour to make a wall of bricks.

PARALLEL BRICK STITCH

This is another simple bargello stitch. It creates bands and can be used to border your work or to create larger, band-based designs; practising it will also help you when you move on to creating the curved stitches.

1 Thread the needle, make a knot and pull through the mono canvas. From your first point of entry count up vertically, leaving 3 meshes, and exit at the 5th mesh. Enter the needle in the next column, 5 meshes down, which is also to the immediate right of your original entry point. Pull the thread.

2 Repeat the step of exiting the needle at the 5th mesh up and re-entering at the 5th mesh down on the next column. Pull the thread until flush.

3 Repeat the same action to the end of the design. You should now see a neat, solid band of stitches appearing; try to keep the tension even throughout by pulling only until the yarn is flush with the mono canvas.

4 Keep repeating step 2 for the required number of stitches. You can repeat the row underneath in the same or another colour to make more bands of colour.

CURVE STITCH

Used frequently in motif-based designs, curve stitch is essential for tackling many of the intermediate and complex designs. Similar to Flame Stitch (see page 21), it is formed of a series of parallel and climbing stitches. Once mastered, you can use it to create circles and ovals that vary in size and dimension.

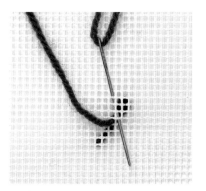

1 Thread the needle, make a knot and pull through the mono canvas. From your first point of entry, count up vertically, leaving 3 meshes, and exit at the 5th mesh. Enter the needle in the next column, 5 meshes down from your exit point. This will bring the needle point out 1 mesh to the right of the first entry point.

2 Pull the thread flush and repeat three times. On the fifth stitch, enter the needle at the 3rd mesh down and not the 5th. You should now have four parallel stitches with the fifth begun in the next column at the centre of the previous stitch.

3 Repeat the steps to make three parallel stitches, ending stitches one, two and three at the 5th mesh up and beginning stitch four at the 3rd mesh down, as with the previous series.

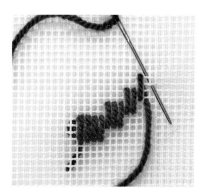

4 Make a pair of parallel stitches, as before. Repeat to make two climbing pairs in total.

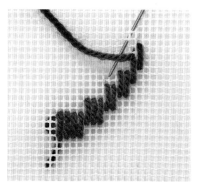

5 Make a pair of climbing brick stitches, continuing upwards. Now enter the needle 3 meshes down to the left. This will bring your needle out at the top of the previous stitch. Exit the needle 5 meshes up and re-enter 3 meshes down to the left.

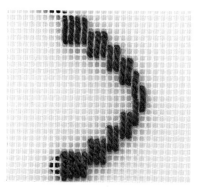

6 Repeat steps 1–4 in reverse and to the left. The pattern of parallels upwards will be two pairs, a trio, and a four.

SCOTTISH STITCH

Scottish stitch is slightly unusual as it is worked over even numbers rather than odd. Composed of a series of straight stitches to form a diamond, this attractive canvas-work stitch is excellent for filling in and creates a quilted effect. Scottish stitch can be worked vertically or diagonally across the canvas, but the principles remain the same.

1 Thread the needle, make a knot and pull through the mono canvas. From the entry point, count up 2 meshes to the 4th mesh, exit the needle and enter one column to the right and 1 mesh up.

2 Pull the thread flush. Count down 4 meshes to the 6th mesh to exit the needle, and enter it one column to the right and 1 mesh down.

3 Count up 6 meshes to the 8th mesh to exit the needle. Enter the needle one column to the right and 1 mesh down.

4 Mirror the previous stitch by counting down 4 meshes to the 6th mesh where you exit the needle and enter in the next column to the right, 1 mesh up from the bottom of your last stitch.

5 To complete, count up 2 meshes to the 4th mesh, exit the needle and pull the thread flush.

6 Begin the next stitch on top of the central and longest part of the previous one. Again, start the stitch with the narrowest edge and work across. You will be able to check your work by noticing that the columns read 4 mesh/8 mesh and 6 mesh/6 mesh vertically throughout the pattern.

7 For the next stitch, working horizontally from the first one, remember that you have already worked the first part of this stitch as it is also the last part of the previous one. Therefore, your next move across is a 6-mesh stitch (followed by an 8, then a 6 and a 4).

LEAF STITCH

Both a feature and a filler stitch, leaf stitch is a challenging way to stretch your skills and make a forest of textured delight. Rewarding in finish and versatile in use, with this stitch you can make rows, columns and borders, as well as fill large background areas.

1 Thread the needle, make a knot and pull through the mono canvas at least 10 meshes up, as this will be the top of your first leaf. From here, exit the needle 2 meshes down at mesh 4. You will continue to return to this central line throughout. Enter the needle one column to the right and 1 mesh down.

2 Exit the needle at the 5th mesh down on the central line. There is a missed mesh between the end of the last stitch and the end of this one. Mirror this on the left side.

3 Moving one column right and 1 mesh down from the start of the last step, enter the needle and exit at the 7th mesh down the central line. Mirror this on the left side.

4 Start by again moving one column right and 1 mesh down from the start of the last step and return to the central line at the 8th mesh down on the central line. Mirror this on the left side.

5 This time, staying in the same column but 1 mesh down from where the last step started, bring the needle to the 9th mesh down on the central line, then mirror on the other side. Repeat this step twice to make three parallel diagonal lines.

6 To begin the next leaf, start at the 7th mesh across and again work downwards, following steps 1–5.

7 To work the upper layers, the central line must be in the column where the lower leaves meet each other at their sides. Remember to start 10 meshes up from the base of the new leaf.

FLAME STITCH

Flame stitch is a bargello icon; also known as Florentine stitch, it is the most used and recognised staple of the art. Introducing for the first time a series of climbing and parallel stitches, this is where the fun really starts.

1 Thread the needle, make a knot and pull through the mono canvas. From the point of entry, count up vertically and exit at the 5th mesh. Enter the needle in the next column, 3 meshes down from your exit point. This will be adjacent to the centre of the first part. Pull the thread.

2 Count up 3 meshes and exit at the 5th mesh. Enter again in the next column, 3 meshes down and adjacent to the centre of the last stitch. Pull the thread through and repeat until there are four climbing single stitches.

3 Repeat a 5th time, but this time entering at the 5th mesh down and not the 3rd, bringing you to the right-hand side of the beginning of this fifth stitch. Pull the thread.

4 Exit the needle at the 5th mesh above to make a parallel stitch, entering this time at the 3rd mesh down on the next column. Pull the thread.

5 Make two parallel stitches following the pattern of 'in at 5 meshes down and out at 5 meshes up', then make a 3rd parallel stitch, but this time entering at 3 meshes down and not 5.

6 Make two parallel stitches of 5 meshes each and then enter the needle 3 meshes down from the end of the previous stitch.

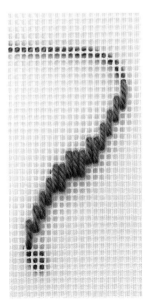

7 Make four climbing single stitches as shown in steps 1 and 2. Continue the pattern by mirroring the stitches you have already completed, working down the canvas (see also page 44).

HUNGARIAN STITCH

Hungarian stitch consists of two different sizes of stitches used together to make a herringbone shape. It is a complex stitch – although once mastered, it can become addictive – and highly versatile, as it can be used in layered rows that tessellate or to create intricate motifs for standout pieces.

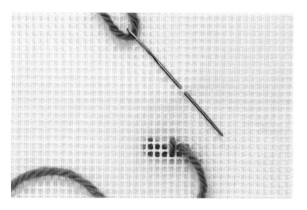

1 Thread the needle, make a knot and pull through the mono canvas. Count up to the 3rd mesh and exit the needle. Re-enter in the next column at the 2nd mesh down, exiting at the 9th mesh up, then re-enter in the next column at the 2nd mesh down.

2 Exit the needle at the 3rd mesh up and re-enter in the next column at the 2nd mesh down.

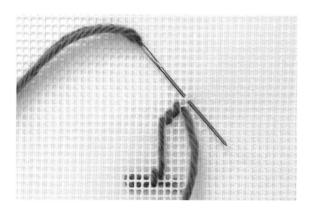

3 Repeat twice to make three climbing stitches of 3 meshes, moving upwards and to the right, ending the third stitch at its centre in the next column.

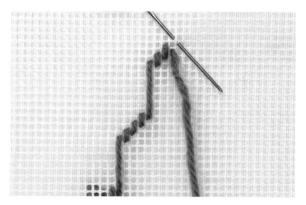

4 Make another 9-mesh stitch, enter the needle 2 meshes down and to the right, then make three smaller 3-mesh climbing stitches (as shown in step 3).

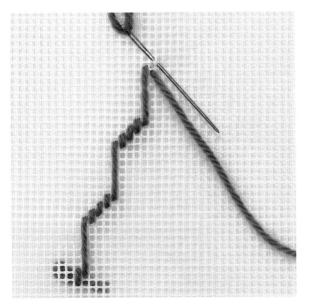

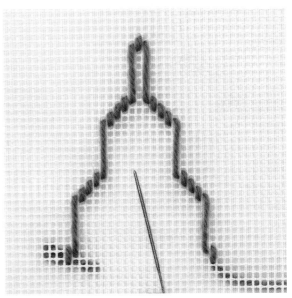

5 Count upwards to make another 9-mesh stitch followed by a 3-mesh stitch, then entering at the 2nd mesh down in the next column. You are now at the top of your herringbone shape and from here will be climbing downwards to the right.

6 Continue the pattern by mirroring the stitches you have already completed, working down the canvas.

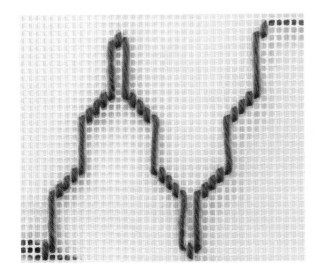

7 Begin the next herringbone in the next column by making a 9-mesh stitch from the 2nd mesh down of the final 3-mesh stitch.

HOW TO MAKE A SWATCH

Now you know the stitches, are you ready to start your bargello project? Before you fire up that needle, here are a few words of advice. Always check where the first stitch is: the edge, the centre or the bottom of the canvas. Keep checking your lines and, above all, enjoy!

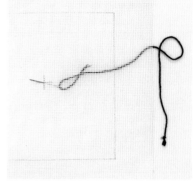

CHOOSE THE DESIGN
The starting place for any project is to work out what you want to do and are able to achieve. Assess your skill level and how much yarn you have. It is a good idea to start with a small number of yarn colours and build up to complex designs with more colours as you gain experience.

PLANNING
Once you have your canvas, plan out the size and shape of your design using a pencil and ruler. Mark the centre point, your planned starting point and a border for the edge. Use a ruler throughout to check lines and distances; for this reason, a clear ruler is highly recommended.

STARTING
Measure out a length of yarn up to approximately 45cm (18in) in standard yarn (shorter for doubled, lurex or finer yarns, as they are more prone to tangling) and thread the needle. Get your canvas firmly in place, using a hoop or frame if preferred. Tie a knot and start sewing.

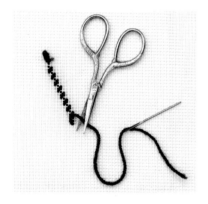

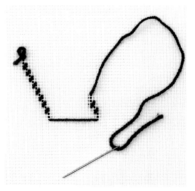

FINISHING
When your tapestry is complete, first block it with a steam iron (see page 13), then prepare it for display (depending on the intended use). One of the easiest ways to do this is to mount it on a ready-made canvas frame, using a staple gun or thumb tacks to secure it.

DURING
There are two schools of thought on yarn changes: tie off or carry across? It's your decision entirely. Tying off can cause tension issues and be tricky to undo in an unpick; carrying across can also get into a tangle when you catch an old yarn and bring it through the canvas with the current yarn.

FIXING MISTAKES

Mistakes are common and frequent. Never get upset about them; they're all fixable. Use your ruler to look at your lines and identify the start of the issue. Unpick using your needle and scissors if necessary to slowly take out the yarn, so as not to warp the canvas. If the mistake is small, you can sometimes get away with overstitching the problem, but this is only for tiny issues.

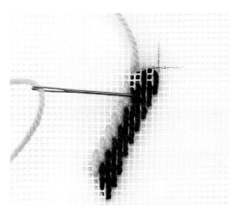

Here, in the middle line of climbing brick stitches, the sixth stitch has overreached by 1 mesh. This is easily corrected in the top line by continuing to stitch in line with the brick stitch pattern and then sewing over the incorrect stitches.

YARN QUANTITIES

A rule of thumb when estimating yarn quantities: A sampler of 22 x 22cm (9 x 9in) of plain stitching in the same yarn (using 10CT mono canvas) has an approximate coverage of 30g (1½oz). However you will need to add around 20 percent for tying off, tangles and changes of direction in stitching. This amount will vary depending on the size of the canvas you use; the finer the gauge, the more yarn it will absorb.

1 Correcting the same error, this time cut into the stitch two stitches after the incorrect stitch, using some sharp scissors.

2 Then unpick to before the error, using your tapestry needle to gently tease out the yarn. Tie the yarn at the back once fixed.

CHAPTER 2

THE
DESIGNS

We have chosen our very favourite bargello designs here; some are traditional patterns and some we have composed ourselves. In every design we have chosen colours that we love and colourways that inspire us from art, décor, fashion and nature. An absolute feast of bold designs and vibrant colour to get your needle humming!

EASY

Zigzag
pages 36–37

Zigzag variation 1
page 38

Zigzag variation 2
page 39

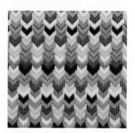

Zigzag variation 3
page 42

Zigzag variation 4
page 42

Zigzag fancy yarn
page 43

Flame
pages 44–45

Flame variation 1
page 46

Flame variation 2
page 47

Flame variation 3
page 48

Flame variation 4
page 49

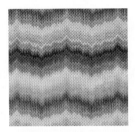

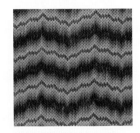

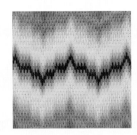

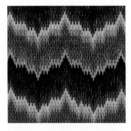

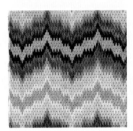

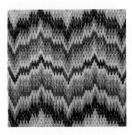

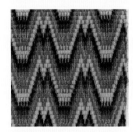

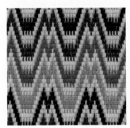

INTERMEDIATE

Pomegranates
pages 68–69

Pomegranates variation 1
page 70

Pomegranates variation 2
page 71

Pomegranates variation 3
page 74

Pomegranates variation 4
page 74

Basket Weave
pages 76–77

Basket Weave variation 1
page 78

Basket Weave variation 2
page 79

Basket Weave variation 3
page 80

Basket Weave variation 4
page 81

Basket Weave fancy yarn
page 82

Boxed Hungarian Point
pages 84–85

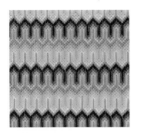

Boxed Hungarian Point
variation 1
page 86

Boxed Hungarian Point
variation 2
page 87

Boxed Hungarian Point
variation 3
page 88

Boxed Hungarian Point
variation 4
page 89

Boxed Hungarian Point
fancy yarn
page 90

Lollipops
pages 92–93

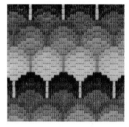

Lollipops variation 1
page 94

Lollipops variation 2
page 95

Lollipops variation 3
page 98

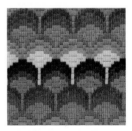

Lollipops variation 4
page 98

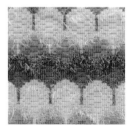

Lollipops fancy yarn
page 99

ADVANCED

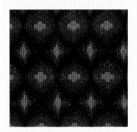

Retro
pages 102–103

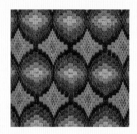

Retro variation 1
page 104

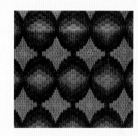

Retro variation 2
page 105

Retro variation 3
page 108

Retro variation 4
page 108

Traditional Hungarian Point
pages 110–111

Traditional Hungarian Point
variation 1
page 112

Traditional Hungarian Point
variation 2
page 113

Traditional Hungarian Point
variation 3
page 116

Traditional Hungarian Point
variation 4
page 116

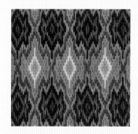

Lanterns
pages 118–119

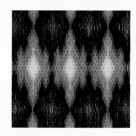

Lanterns variation 1
page 120

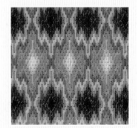

Lanterns variation 2
page 121

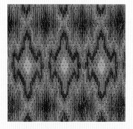

Lanterns variation 3
page 122

Lanterns variation 4
page 123

Lanterns fancy yarn
page 124

TAKING BARGELLO FURTHER
EDGES AND BORDERS, TEXTURAL, FREESTYLING

Spiral Bands
pages 128–129

Crossed Spiral Bands
pages 130–131

Diagonal Stripes
pages 132–133

Chains
pages 134–135

Fused Spiral Bands
pages 136–137

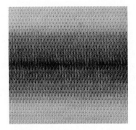

Climbing Brick Stitch
pages 138–139

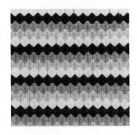

Leaf Stitch
pages 140–141

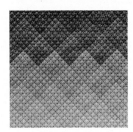

Double Cross Stitch
pages 142–143

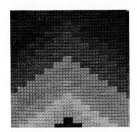

Pyramids
pages 144–145

Hexagons
pages 146–147

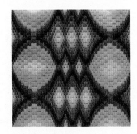

Blazing Baubles
pages 148–149

Reflected Hungarian Point
Motif
pages 150–151

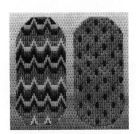

Lozenges
pages 152–153

Honeycombs
pages 154–155

EASY

We start with four exciting patterns, all of which are worked in rows across the canvas. From the impossibly versatile Zigzag to the pure geometry of Peaks, via the eternal Flame – an absolute must for any bargello fan – and the moody and romantic Aurora Borealis.

Featured stitches
Climbing Brick Stitch (see page 16)
Parallel Brick Stitch (see page 17)

ZIGZAG

This is a very basic zigzag stitch, also known as Byzantine stitch. It is ideal for anyone trying bargello for the first time. The pattern is so versatile: it can be done in stripes or fading colours, or split into sections, transforming the stitch into something completely different. You can sew it vertically, horizontally or diagonally. This pattern works well with a sweet palette of sweet shop colours, but the potential for colour play is endless.

PATTERN REPEAT

This design is done over 5 meshes (in at 1, out at 5) and is made up of a repeating simple straight stitch. Start a little way up from the bottom of the canvas and then work your way up.

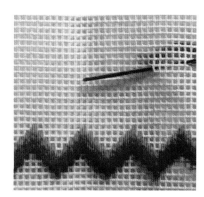

1 Complete the first line of stitches along the width of the canvas.

2 Repeat step 1 with white yarn for the line above.

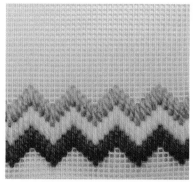

3 Complete each row along the width of the canvas, adding a row of white between each coloured row.

YOU WILL NEED

Yarn 5g (¼oz) per colour and 10g (½oz) of white, using a mix of acrylics (DK)

Mono canvas (10CT) 22 x 22cm (9 x 9in), leaving a 2cm (¾in) border around the edges

Tapestry needle

- ● Magenta
- ○ White
- ○ Pale blue
- ● Egg yolk
- ● Pastel pink
- ● Tangy orange
- ● Royal blue

- ○ Turquoise
- ● Burgundy
- ○ Lime green
- ● Electric blue
- ● Bubblegum pink
- ○ Pear

Choosing bold hues, alternated with a dramatic white stripe, is ideal if you want to use up any odds and ends in your yarn basket.

ZIGZAG

VARIATION 1

YOU WILL NEED
Yarn 5g (¼oz) per colour, using a mix of acrylics (DK)
Mono canvas (10CT) 22 x 22cm (9 x 9in), leaving a 2cm (¾in) border around the edges
Tapestry needle

- Pale pink
- Frosty pink
- Candy pink
- Candy floss
- Dusky rose
- Pink
- Paradise pink
- Magenta
- Bubblegum pink
- Deep musky pink
- Deep rose

All the pinks in a traditional bargello fade are stepped to create a dusky sunset of lush romantic tones. We suggest that you select between six and eleven pinks that fade from light to dark to create this striking effect. We have used eleven shades in this sample, but you can choose however many you like.

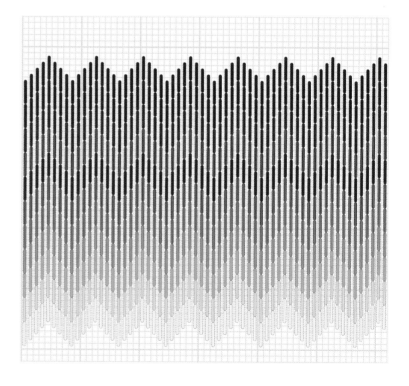

VARIATION 2

YOU WILL NEED

Yarn 5g (¼oz) per colour, using a mix of acrylics (DK)

Mono canvas (10CT) 22 x 22cm (9 x 9in), leaving a 2cm (¾in) border around the edges

Tapestry needle

- Pale peach
- Musky peach
- Tangy orange
- Tangerine
- Pale blue
- Aqua
- Electric blue
- Royal blue
- Pale pink
- Pink
- Bubblegum pink
- Magenta

A zesty stripe series in popping pinks, cool blues and tasty tangerines, featuring an even shade fade of four colours in each colour section.

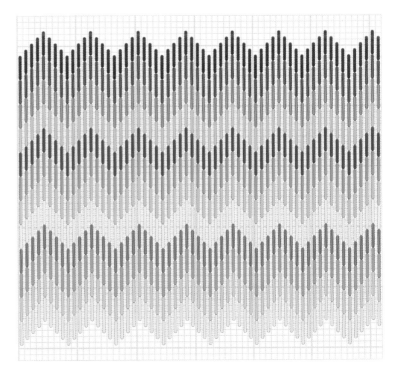

ZIGZAG \ VARIATION 3 (pattern)
see page 42

ZIGZAG \ VARIATION 4 (pattern)
see page 42

ZIGZAG

VARIATION 3
see page 40

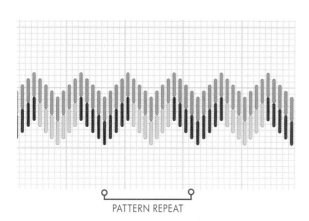

PATTERN REPEAT

YOU WILL NEED
Yarn 5g (¼oz) per colour and 10g (½oz)
of white, using a mix of acrylics (DK)
Mono canvas (10CT) 22 x 22cm
(9 x 9in), leaving a 2cm (¾in) border
around the edges
Tapestry needle

- Lime green
- ● Burgundy
- ○ White
- Pale blue
- Tangy orange
- Electric blue
- Egg yolk
- Magenta
- Dusky rose
- Pear
- Bright lemon

VARIATION 4
see page 41

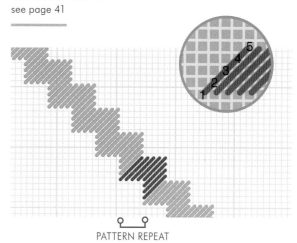

PATTERN REPEAT

YOU WILL NEED
Yarn 5g (¼oz) per colour and 10g (½oz)
of white, using a mix of acrylics (DK)
Mono canvas (10CT) 22 x 22cm
(9 x 9in), leaving a 2cm (¾in) border
around the edges
Tapestry needle

- Magenta
- Deep turquoise
- Neon yellow
- Pink
- Tangy orange
- Aqua blue
- Royal blue

You can mix and match any two alternating colours
in a row. Once you have embroidered all rows, go
back and fill in the gaps at the top and bottom of
the canvas, following the finished sample.

FANCY YARN

Here, the Zigzag design (see pages 36–37) is worked over an autumn-inspired palette of muted fruit shades of greens, golds, oranges and purples, all with a little extra sparkle! The stitch size and the order of the colours are varied to create a random look in a uniform pattern.

- Jewel with glitter
- Burnt orange with glitter
- Mustard with glitter
- Mauve with glitter
- Emerald with glitter
- Lilac with glitter
- Olive with glitter

Featured stitches
Climbing Brick Stitch (see page 16)
Parallel Brick Stitch (see page 17)
Flame Stitch (see page 21)

FLAME

Flame uses traditional Flame Stitch, sometimes called
Florentine stitch, which underpins most bargello designs.
Once this is mastered, other stitches are much easier to learn.

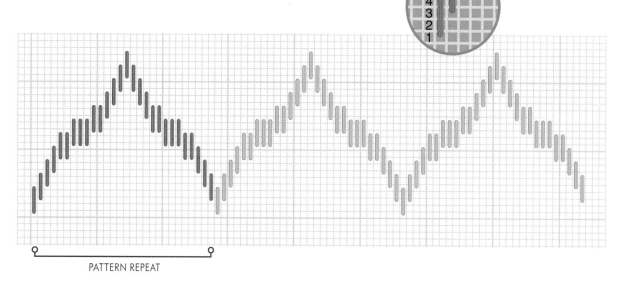

PATTERN REPEAT

This sample uses seven shades, sewn over 5 meshes. Start a little way up from
the bottom of the canvas and work your way up.

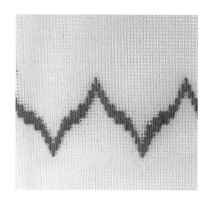

1 Complete the first row of stitches
along the width of the canvas.

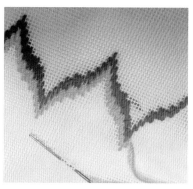

2 Once you have stitched the first
row, repeat, changing colour as
and when for each row.

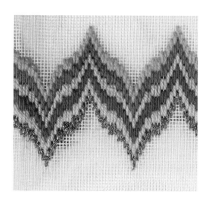

3 Complete each row along the
width of the canvas.

Once you have embroidered all rows,
go back and fill in the gaps at the top
and bottom of the canvas, following the
finished sample.

YOU WILL NEED

Yarn 20g (1oz) per colour, using a mix of acrylics (DK) and gold lurex 2 ply (doubled up to make 4 ply)

Mono canvas (10CT) 22 x 22cm (9 x 9in), leaving a 7cm (2¾in) border around the edges

Tapestry needle

- Coral
- Pale lemon
- Gold lurex
- Mulberry
- Tangy orange
- Orange
- Pale lilac

A fiery working of a simple stitch whose rise and fall creates elegant structures that appear complex (due to colour changes), but are actually simple to achieve.

FLAME

VARIATION 1

YOU WILL NEED

Yarn 5g (¼oz) per colour, using a mix of acrylics (DK) and gold lurex 2 ply (doubled up to make 4 ply)

Mono canvas (10CT) 22 x 22cm (9 x 9in), leaving a 7cm (2¾in) border around the edges

Tapestry needle

- Gold lurex
- Pink
- Magenta
- Currant
- Claret
- Pale lemon
- Mustard

Inspired by the colours of the Moroccan bazaar, this design features deep pinks and opulent golds in a regular bargello Flame.

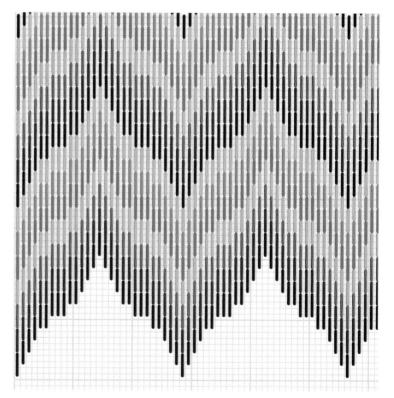

VARIATION 2

YOU WILL NEED

Yarn 5g (¼oz) per colour, using a mix of acrylics (DK) and gold lurex 2 ply (doubled up to make 4 ply)

Mono canvas (10CT) 22 x 22cm (9 x 9in), leaving a 7cm (2¾in) border around the edges

Tapestry needle

- Gold lurex
- Burgundy
- Lime green
- Pear
- Olive with glitter
- Mint
- Orange

From deep burgundy to a spectrum of limes and glitz, this irregular Flame evokes all the drama and glamour of a Bollywood movie set. Follow the pattern for the main design, but work some colours over two or three repeats, as per the chart.

FLAME

VARIATION 3

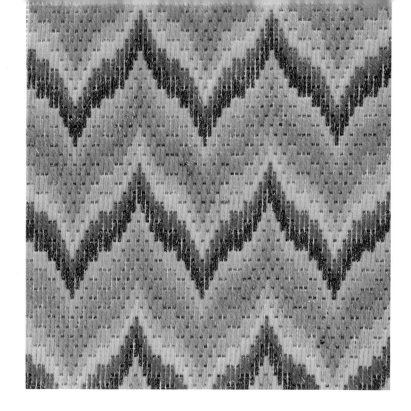

YOU WILL NEED

Yarn 5g (¼oz) per colour, using a mix of acrylics (DK)

Mono canvas (10CT) 22 x 22cm (9 x 9in), leaving a 7cm (2¾in) border around the edges

Tapestry needle

- Orange lurex
- Sunshine yellow
- Mustard
- Corn cob with glitter
- Vintage peach
- Chartreuse
- Yellow green
- Olive with glitter

Inspired by the romantic and lush landscapes of Ireland and by the colours of the Irish flag, but with a little extra twinkle.

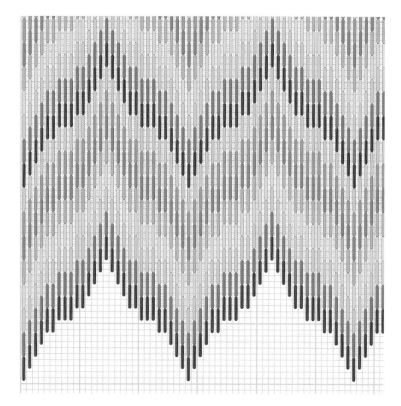

VARIATION 4

YOU WILL NEED

Yarn 5g (¼oz) per colour, using a mix of acrylics (DK) and gold lurex 2 ply (doubled up to make 4 ply)

Mono canvas (10CT) 22 x 22cm (9 x 9in), leaving a 7cm (2¾in) border around the edges

Tapestry needle

- Blackberry
- Purple
- Mauve
- Gold lurex
- Lavender

Warm, decadent evening tones in deep, rich, plummy purples, highlighted with gold, make this luxe palette sing and sparkle.

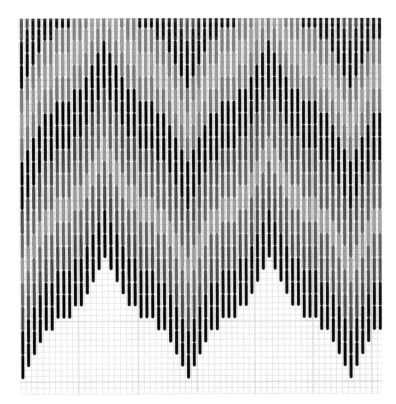

Featured stitches
Climbing Brick Stitch (see page 16)
Parallel Brick Stitch (see page 17)

AURORA BOREALIS

A traditional rendering of a bargello staple, Aurora Borealis captures the polar lights in stitch. In this sample, we use mid-toned pastels to create a gentle fade from dark to light and light to dark.

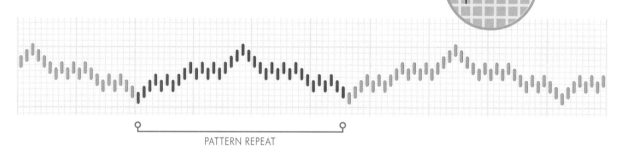

PATTERN REPEAT

This sample is worked over 3 meshes.
Create the highest peak of the design,
starting halfway up the canvas on the left and
working towards the right-hand side.

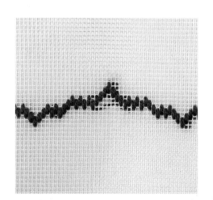

1 Follow the pattern to the end of the row.

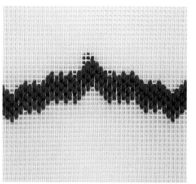

2 Change yarn colour and complete the next two rows of stitches, following the line above and below your first line and starting at the left-hand side.

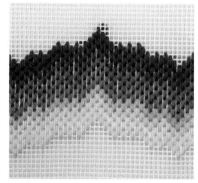

3 Keep repeating step 2, above and below, changing the colour of the yarn for every row.

YOU WILL NEED

Yarn 5g (¼oz) per colour,
using a mix of acrylics (DK)
Mono canvas (10CT) 22 x
22cm (9 x 9in), leaving a 2cm
(¾in) border around the edges
Tapestry needle

A *selection of*

- 8 Oranges
- 8 Lilacs
- 8 Blues
- 8 Yellows

Colours of twilight meet
colours of sunset in this
deceptively simple, but
sophisticated, array of rich
and pastel tones.

AURORA BOREALIS

VARIATION 1

YOU WILL NEED
Yarn 5g (¼oz) per colour, using a mix of acrylics (DK)
Mono canvas (10CT) 22 x 22cm (9 x 9in), leaving a 2cm (¾in) border around the edges
Tapestry needle

- ● Bright fuchsia
- ● Mustard
- ● Pistachio
- ● Moss
- ● Olive
- ● Dark olive

The lines of bright fuchsia create an electric shock through a selection of greens, graduating to a beautiful but stormy blur. Work all rows from left to right, embroidering the dark olive over three rows and all the other colours over one row.

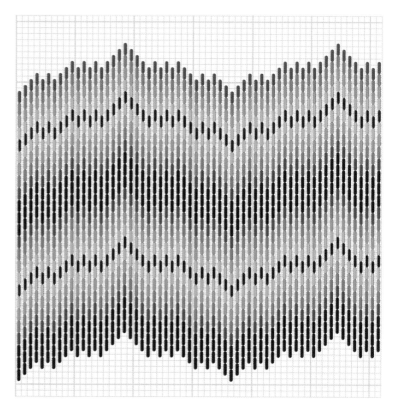

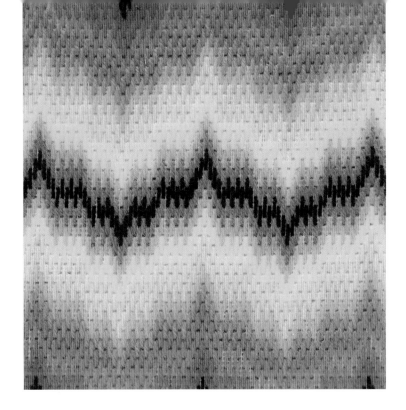

VARIATION 2

YOU WILL NEED

Yarn 5g (¼oz) per colour, using a mix of acrylics (DK)

Mono canvas (10CT) 22 x 22cm (9 x 9in), leaving a 2cm (¾in) border around the edges

Tapestry needle

- ● Dark olive
- ○ Lemongrass
- ◔ Chartreuse
- ◌ Lime green
- ▒ Pale lemon
-   Cream
- ▒ Sunshine
- ◕ Mustard
- ● Tangy orange
- ● Tangerine
- ● Orange
- ● Neon orange

A mix of classic bargello moves in this mirrored Aurora Borealis. The eerie neons against the warm citruses give an atmospheric feel, showcasing the bargello fade at its best. This design is worked over 5 meshes.

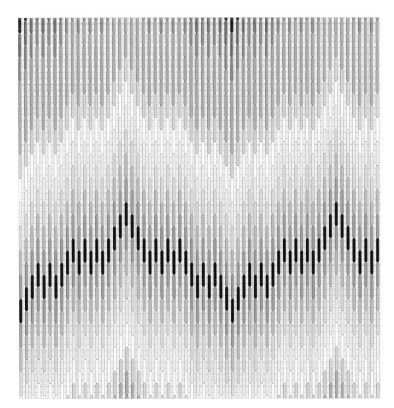

AURORA BOREALIS \ VARIATION 3
see page 56

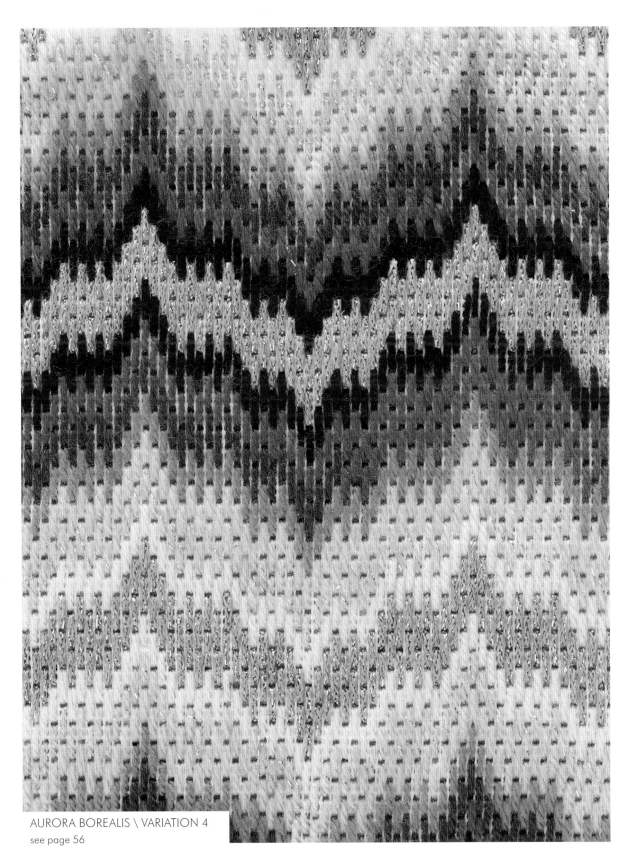

AURORA BOREALIS \ VARIATION 4
see page 56

AURORA BOREALIS

VARIATION 3
see page 54

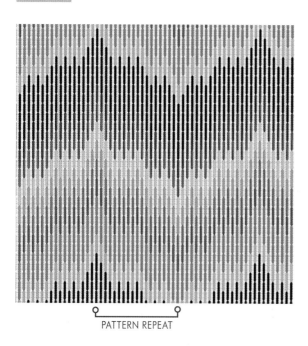

PATTERN REPEAT

VARIATION 4
see page 55

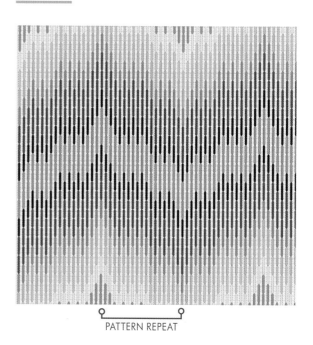

PATTERN REPEAT

YOU WILL NEED
Yarn 5g (¼oz) per colour, using a mix of acrylics (DK)
Mono canvas (10CT) 22 x 22cm (9 x 9in), leaving a 2cm (¾in) border around the edges
Tapestry needle

- Silver lurex
- Forest fruit
- Plum
- Garnet with glitter
- Currant
- Magenta
- Pale pink
- Dusky rose
- Heather
- Party purple
- Jewel with glitter
- Orchid

This Aurora Borealis is worked over a six-shade bargello fade, rather than the traditional four. This luxe landscape in deep swathes of violet and rose is created using a deeper fade of six glamorous shades with bold strikes of magenta and silver to break up the pattern.

YOU WILL NEED
Yarn 5g (¼oz) per colour, using a mix of acrylics (DK)
Mono canvas (10CT) 22 x 22cm (9 x 9in), leaving a 2cm (¾in) border around the edges
Tapestry needle

- Metallic gold
- Chocolate
- Sable
- Chestnut
- Mink
- Pink beige
- Champagne with glitter
- Pale sand

A sandstorm of desert glamour in this brave and dramatic one-colour bargello fade. A sea of sumptuous neutral tones with an iridescent gold horizon.

FANCY YARN

Using a reflected Aurora Borealis design (see Variation 2, on page 53), this piece uses lurex yarns, glittered DKs, and wool to create a textured landscape in blues and golds.

- Blue lurex
- Apricot with cotton fleck
- Old gold
- Copper with glitter
- Chestnut
- Norsk in ice blue
- Airforce blue with glitter
- Navy with glitter
- Royal blue with glitter
- Gold lurex
- Champagne with glitter

Featured stitches
Climbing Brick Stitch (see page 16)
Parallel Brick Stitch (see page 17)

PEAKS

This is a simple yet very effective pattern with structured peaks that create a geometric delight. These are peaks you want to climb – with your needle, of course.

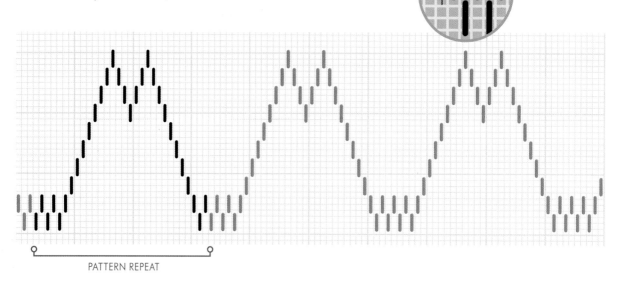

PATTERN REPEAT

This design is worked over 4 meshes (in at mesh 1 and out at 4) from the centre of the canvas.

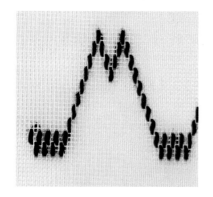

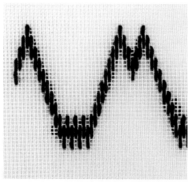

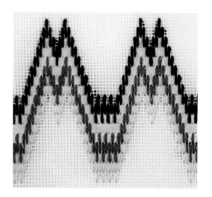

1 Find the approximate central point on the left-hand side of your canvas and, using black yarn, work the pattern to the right-hand side of the canvas.

2 Repeat the entire row underneath the first row, working right to left, again in black.

3 Repeat steps 1 and 2 with the different coloured yarns to complete the pattern.

Once you have embroidered all rows, go back and fill in the gaps at the top and bottom of the canvas, following the finished sample.

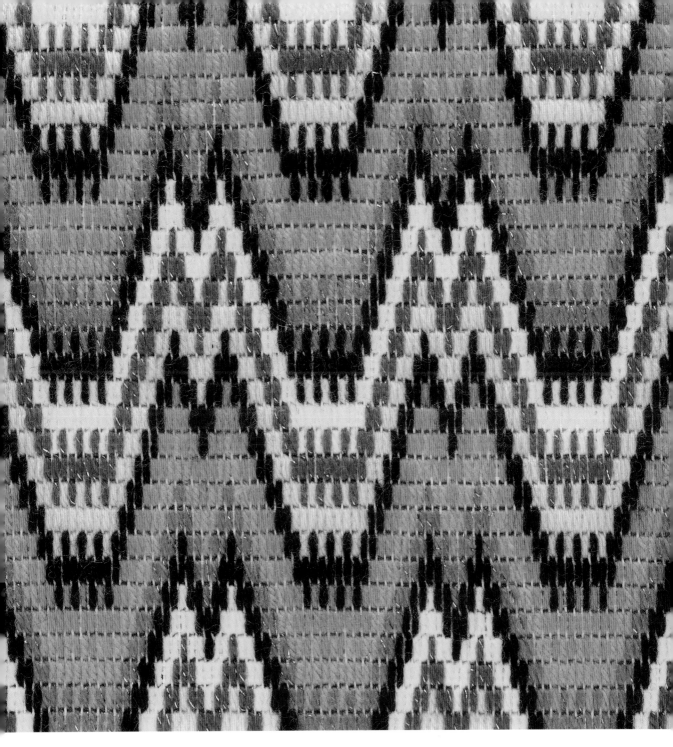

YOU WILL NEED

Yarn 5g (¼oz) per colour, using a mix of acrylics (DK)

Mono canvas (10CT) 22 x 22cm (9 x 9in), leaving a 2cm (¾in) border around the edges

Tapestry needle

- ● Black
- ○ Lime green
- ● Burnt orange with glitter
- ○ Nude
- ● Vibrant orange
- ● Tangy orange
- ● Olive with glitter

This sample is inspired by a Liberty postcard pinned to our studio wall. We have fired up the colour scheme by setting vibrant oranges against black to set this canvas aglow.

PEAKS

VARIATION 1

YOU WILL NEED

Yarn 5g (¼oz) per colour, using a mix of acrylics (DK) and gold lurex 2 ply (doubled up to make 4 ply)

Mono canvas (10CT) 22 x 22cm (9 x 9in), leaving a 2cm (¾in) border around the edges

Tapestry needle

- Gold lurex
- Claret
- Garnet
- Spiced pink
- Magenta
- Royal blue
- Steel blue
- Sky blue
- Turquoise

This work is vibrant and delicious, with pink and blue fades moving from dark to lighter shades, incorporating an accent of gold to illuminate the deep rich intensity of the palette.

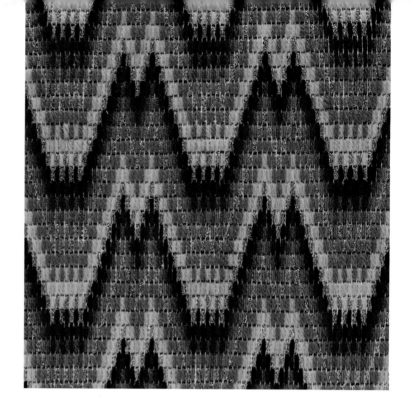

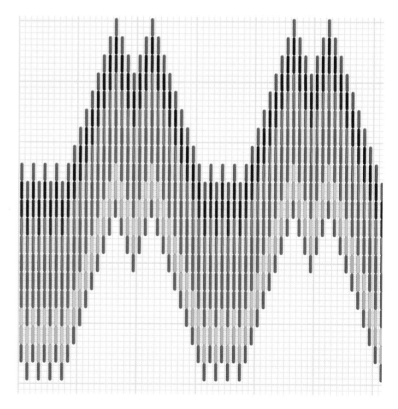

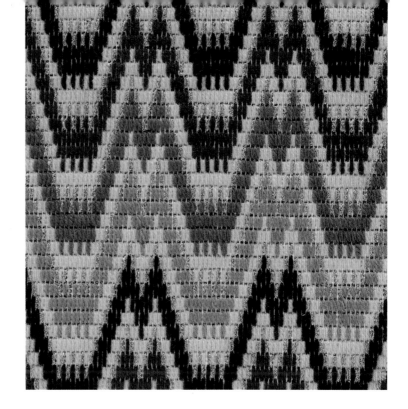

VARIATION 2

YOU WILL NEED

Yarn 5g (¼oz) per colour, using a mix of acrylics (DK) and gold lurex 2 ply (doubled up to make 4 ply)

Mono canvas (10CT) 22 x 22cm (9 x 9in), leaving a 2cm (¾in) border around the edges

Tapestry needle

- ● Gold lurex
- ● Navy
- ● Lemon yellow
- ● Royal blue
- ● Airforce blue
- ● Dark navy

A classic colour combination of yellow and blue, using less predictable tones to add a new twist and colour dimension. The design is highlighted with gold lurex to give a luxurious and richly sophisticated feel.

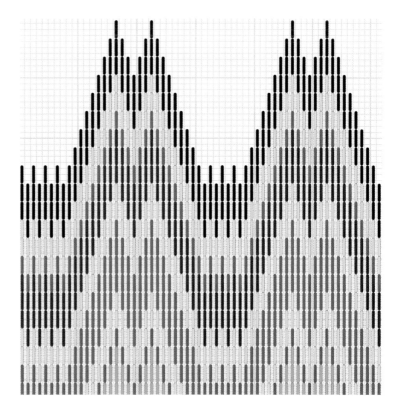

PEAKS

VARIATION 3

YOU WILL NEED

Yarn 5g (¼oz) per colour, using a mix of acrylics (DK)

Mono canvas (10CT) 22 x 22cm (9 x 9in), leaving a 2cm (¾in) border around the edges

Tapestry needle

- Dark teal
- Deep turquoise
- Aqua
- Dark olive
- Army green
- Deep pistachio
- Candy pink
- Pink
- Pale pink
- Plum
- Mauve
- Lilac
- Autumn orange
- Spiced orange
- Peach

This fresh range of colours came to us unexpectedly. We started with the pinks and added colours as we went along, and surprised ourselves with this beautiful palette. It's good to experiment with colours you don't normally expect to go well together. In this design, each colour is worked over one row rather than two.

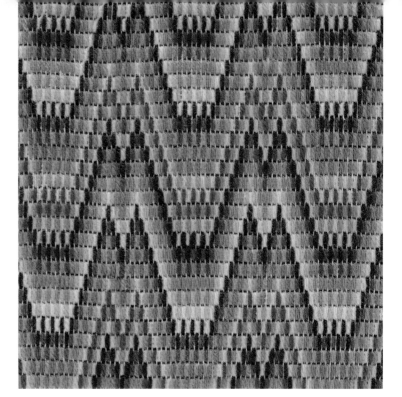

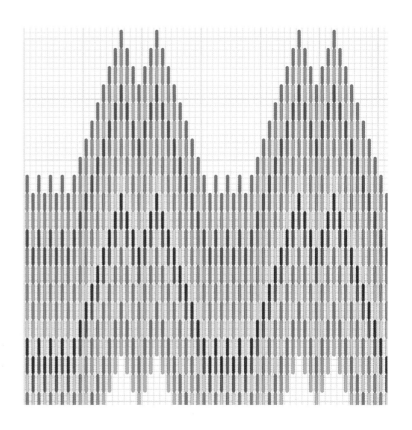

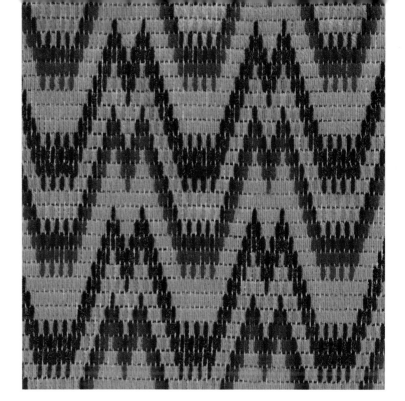

VARIATION 4

YOU WILL NEED

Yarn 5g (¼oz) per colour, using a mix of acrylics (DK) and dark red lurex 2 ply (doubled up to make 4 ply)
Mono canvas (10CT) 22 x 22cm (9 x 9in), leaving a 2cm (¾in) border around the edges
Tapestry needle

- ● Burgundy
- ● Dark red lurex
- ● Claret
- ● Tangy orange
- ● Spiced orange
- ● Light terracotta
- ● Forest fruit
- ● Currant
- ● Raspberry
- ● Neon orange

Dark reds, burgundies and oranges give this design a hot, tangy vibe with a touch of deep red lurex to add sparkle to the overall warm tonality.

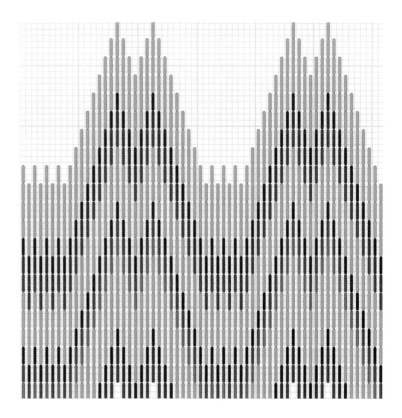

FANCY YARN

Using a Peaks design (see page 58–59), this is a nostalgic piece inspired by 1970s glam rock. Using just three lurex metallics, with matching lines of DK wool between each section, makes for a shimmering version of the Peaks sampler.

● Charcoal
● Lilac lurex
● Royal purple
● Orange lurex
● Dark orange
○ Silver lurex

PEAKS

A striking cushion in the Peaks design repeated at four times the scale and in a cool colour palette. Using a duo canvas for soft furnishings, this design can be used front and back, or just on one side with a complementary fabric.

INTERMEDIATE

The four designs in this section are motif-based and will explore your skills in setting out and repeating a pattern. Pomegranates is an absolute icon of the craft and a must-sew! Basket Weave will help to develop rhythm as the counting becomes a mantra. Both Boxed Hungarian Point and Lollipops introduce using different stitch sizes in the same motif.

Featured stitches
Climbing Brick Stitch (see page 16)
Parallel Brick Stitch (see page 17)
Curve Stitch (see page 18)

POMEGRANATES

The origins of Pomegranates are American rather than Florentine, and they introduce Curve Stitch. There's a colour limit of eight yarns here, so choose your palette first, although colours can be repeated in the diamond-shaped section in the middle if you prefer stripes. The real trick to successful Pomegranates is to set out the outline successfully, then the rest is a lovely form of colouring in the piece with your wools.

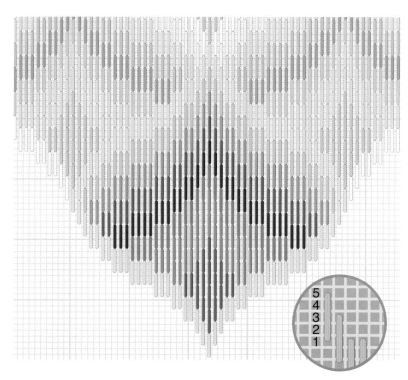

1 Find the centre of the canvas, count 24 meshes to the left of the centre point and enter your needle at the 3rd mesh down from that point (the 2nd being mesh 1) at the back and commence your first 5-mesh stitch. Follow the chart to complete the outline of the Pomegranate.

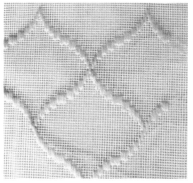

2 Repeat the outline of the Pomegranate to cover as much of the canvas as you wish to use.

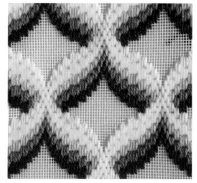

3 Build up your Pomegranates using your eight yarn colours.

YOU WILL NEED

Yarn 40g (2oz) for base diamonds (Pale lemon in this example); 20g (1oz) for each of the other colours (double if you wish to repeat a coloured stripe)

Mono canvas (10CT) 22 x 22cm (9 x 9in), leaving a 2cm (¾in) border around the edges

Tapestry needle

Pale lemon
Lime green
Chartreuse
Cabbage green
Forest green
Gold lurex
Light Prussian blue
Electric blue

Inspired by the eye of a peacock feather, this is a luxe palette straight from nature.

POMEGRANATES

VARIATION 1

YOU WILL NEED
Yarn 40g (2oz) for base
diamonds; 20g (1oz) for each of
the other colours, using a mix of
acrylics (DK)
Mono canvas (10CT) 22 x 22cm
(9 x 9in), leaving a 2cm (¾in)
border around the edges
Tapestry needle

Light peppermint
Sea foam
Magenta
Bubblegum pink
Teal with glitter
Mint
Lilac
Pale lilac

This Pomegranate example has more
contrast than the one on the previous
page. Here, clashing colour contrasts
punch out from the weave. The
inside of the Pomegranate is where
the treasure is and, in the centre
here, the two-tone lilac diamond sits
quietly, leaving the riotous red-pink
combination to make all the noise.

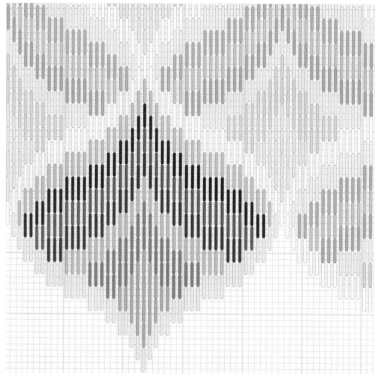

VARIATION 2

YOU WILL NEED
Yarn 40g (2oz) for base diamonds; 20g (1oz) for each of the other colours, using a mix of acrylics (DK)
Mono canvas (10CT) 22 x 22cm (9 x 9in), leaving a 2cm (¾in) border around the edges
Tapestry needle

- Classic yellow
- Navy
- Fluorescent purple
- Cream
- Deep mustard
- Pale lemon
- Fields of gold

These Pomegranates celebrate warm autumn tones using mustard, navy and mauve to create distinct lines and a chic and sophisticated finish.

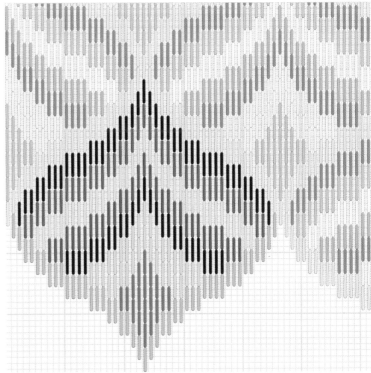

POMEGRANATES \ VARIATION 3
see page 74

POMEGRANATES \ VARIATION 4
see page 74

POMEGRANATES

VARIATION 3

see page 72

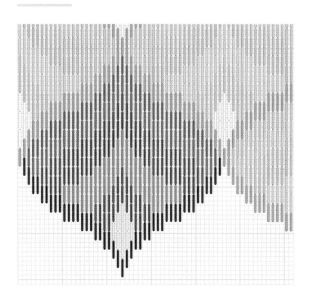

VARIATION 4

see page 73

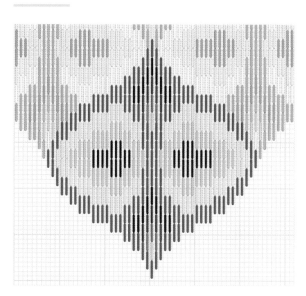

YOU WILL NEED

Yarn 40g (2oz) for base diamonds; 20g (1oz) for each of the other colours, using a mix of acrylics (DK)

Mono canvas (10CT) 22 x 22cm (9 x 9in), leaving a 2cm (¾in) border around the edges

Tapestry needle

- Rust
- Vintage petrol blue
- Mustard
- Fluorescent purple
- Signal red
- Sage green
- Fuchsia
- Neon yellow

An alternative working of Pomegranates where each band of colour is uniquely distinct from the last, inspired by the colours and textiles of the 1970s.

YOU WILL NEED

Yarn 30g (1½oz) Emerald green, 20g (1oz) Royal purple, and 5g (¼oz) for each of the other colours, using a mix of acrylics (DK)

Mono canvas (10CT) 22 x 22cm (9 x 9in), leaving a 2cm (¾in) border around the edges

Tapestry needle

- Emerald green
- Pale lime
- Candy green
- Royal purple
- Currant
- Fluorescent purple
- Lilac

This is a new play on Pomegranates, using the exact same outline but with a few simple stitch changes to the inner section to create a whole new pattern.

POMEGRANATES

Bright spring Pomegranates transform this stool in a pastel palette highlighted with accents of hot pink. This is a simple case of making a circle and either one band or grafting a number of smaller bands together to make the edge. Measure carefully.

Featured stitches
Climbing Brick Stitch (see page 16)
Parallel Brick Stitch (see page 17)

BASKET WEAVE

This pattern is created with Parallel Brick Stitch, in pairs and crossing in diagonal rows to form a woven effect.

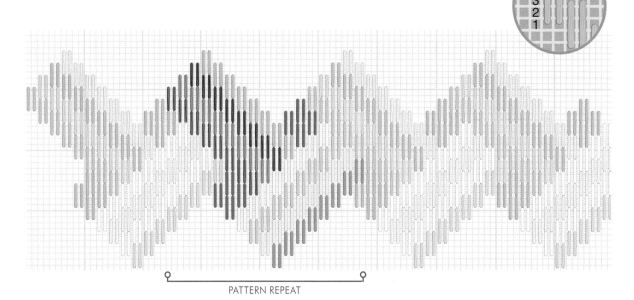

PATTERN REPEAT

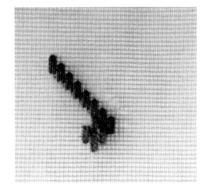

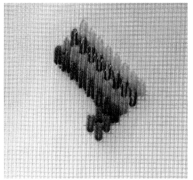

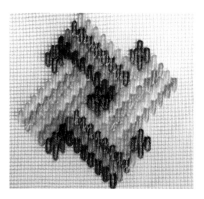

1 Mark the centre of your canvas, and over that sew a cross of four pairs of stitches over 5 meshes. At the centre of the right-hand side of the cross, make a pair of stitches in a new thread and move upwards diagonally from the centre of each pair until you have eight pairs of stitches.

2 Follow this row (starting slightly to the right each time) with three rows above, changing the colour for each row, as shown.

3 Returning to the cross, repeat the series of stripes in the yellow yarns. Sew a new cross at the intersection of the pink and yellow bands of colour, and continue steps 1–3 until the canvas is completed.

YOU WILL NEED

Yarn 5g (¼oz) per colour using a mix of acrylics (DK)

Mono canvas (10CT) 22 x 22cm (9 x 9in), leaving a 2cm (¾in) border around the edges

Tapestry needle

- Scouting green
- Raspberry
- Pink
- Raspberry with cotton fleck
- Pale pink
- Primrose
- Apricot with cotton fleck
- Bright lemon
- Sunshine gold

This is a bright Basket Weave bargello in popping summer shades of raspberry and apricot, accented with a grassy green to add to the 'back to nature' feel.

BASKET WEAVE

VARIATION 1

YOU WILL NEED
Yarn 5g (¼oz) per colour, using a mix of acrylics (DK)
Mono canvas (10CT) 22 x 22cm (9 x 9in), leaving a 2cm (¾in) border around the edges
Tapestry needle

- Scouting green
- Burnt orange
- Tangy orange
- Tangerine
- Sand
- Fields of gold
- Mustard
- Golden sultana
- Pineapple

A burst of citrus brights in grapefruit and tangerine shades in a classic bargello fade.

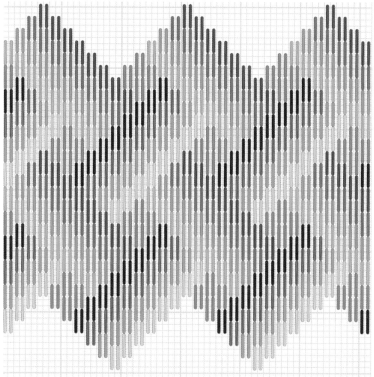

VARIATION 2

YOU WILL NEED

Yarn 5g (¼oz) per colour, using a mix of acrylics (DK)

Mono canvas (10CT) 22 x 22cm (9 x 9in), leaving a 2cm (¾in) border around the edges

Tapestry needle

- Gold lurex
- Peach kiss
- Baby pink
- Tangerine
- Raspberry
- Nude
- Pale pink
- Tangy orange
- Party purple

This is an alternative interpretation of Basket Weave. Here, colours are stacked in blocks of bright shades and mirrored with their muted counterparts for a fun fruity palette.

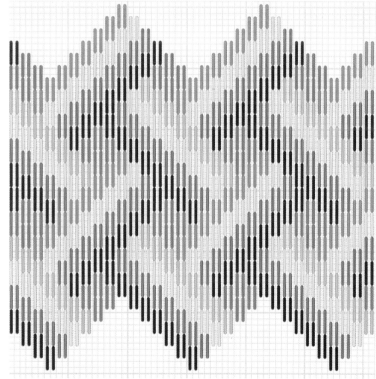

BASKET WEAVE

VARIATION 3

YOU WILL NEED

Yarn 5g (¼oz) per colour, using a mix of acrylics (DK)

Mono canvas (10CT) 22 x 22cm (9 x 9in), leaving a 2cm (¾in) border around the edges

Tapestry needle

- ● Sunshine gold
-   Cream
- ● Tortilla
- ● Softest beige
- ● Golden brown
- ● Chocolate
- ● Bottle brown
- ● Fawn
- ● Mink
- ● Primrose

NOTE: On this design, the colour of the crosses repeats diagonally, but alternates horizontally.

A traditional Basket Weave design in natural tones, faded for a rustic feel and interspersed with pockets of morning and afternoon sunshine.

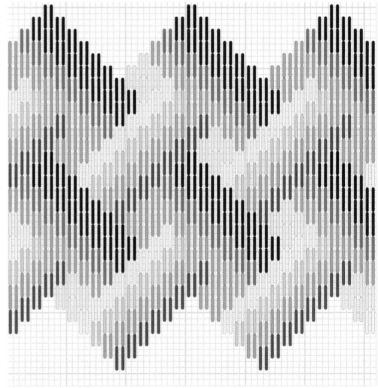

VARIATION 4

YOU WILL NEED

Yarn 5g (¼oz) per colour, using a mix of acrylics (DK)

Mono canvas (10CT) 22 x 22cm (9 x 9in), leaving a 2cm (¾in) border around the edges

Tapestry needle

- Blue lurex
- Ladybird
- Sunshine yellow

A bold Basket Weave in primary colours demonstrates the simplicity of the design. Inspired by a childhood love of Lego, it uses solid blocks of colour to create the impression of woven stripes.

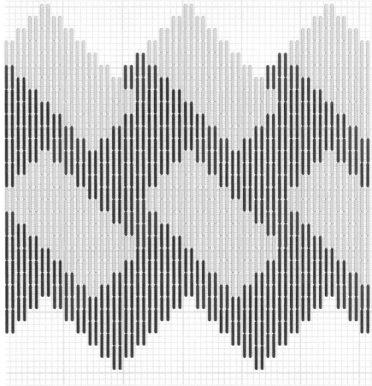

FANCY YARN

This Basket Weave design (see page 76) is intended to complement the energetic colours of the feathered multi yarn used in the crosses. The feathered and glittery yarns bring texture and glamour to the design. Note that all of the glitter threads used here are doubled up in thickness for better coverage.

- Feathered multi
- Electric blue
- Metallic orange
- Neon pink
- Metallic yellow
- Metallic turquoise
- Tangy orange
- Metallic pink
- Marigold

BASKET WEAVE

A summery working of Basket Weave to make a dramatic and unique lampshade. Get an accurate measurement of the circumference of the lampshade before starting and choose a lighter colour palette for this project. Mono canvas is recommended for stiffness and less opacity.

Featured stitches
Climbing Brick Stitch (see page 16)
Parallel Brick Stitch (see page 17)
Hungarian Stitch (see pages 22–23)

BOXED HUNGARIAN POINT

This is the simplest and tidiest of the Hungarian Point designs and a lovely introduction to using long and short stitches in the same design. It is usually worked using nine colours, but can be simplified to five. The key to this design is to start with the scalloped line (here in gold lurex) and then follow the top of it for the next four rows to create the 'boxes'.

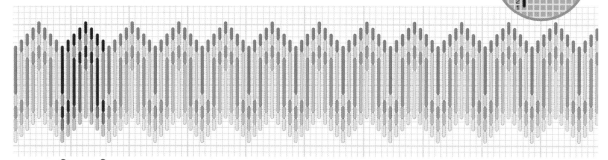

PATTERN REPEAT

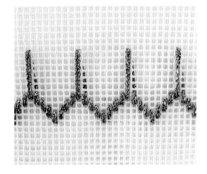

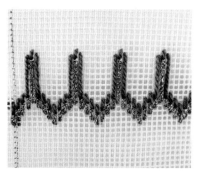

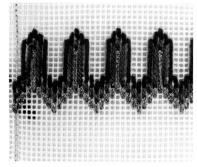

1 Start from the left-hand side of the canvas, approximately halfway up. Make four small brick stitches over 3 meshes, then one long stitch over 9 meshes, followed by three brick stitches climbing down. This will make an inverted Y-shape. Repeat this to the end of the row.

2 Changing the yarn colour and stitching directly on top of the first row, follow it, changing the length of the stitches, as shown in the chart.

3 Change the yarn colour three more times to create three more rows and continue steps 1–3 until the design fills the canvas.

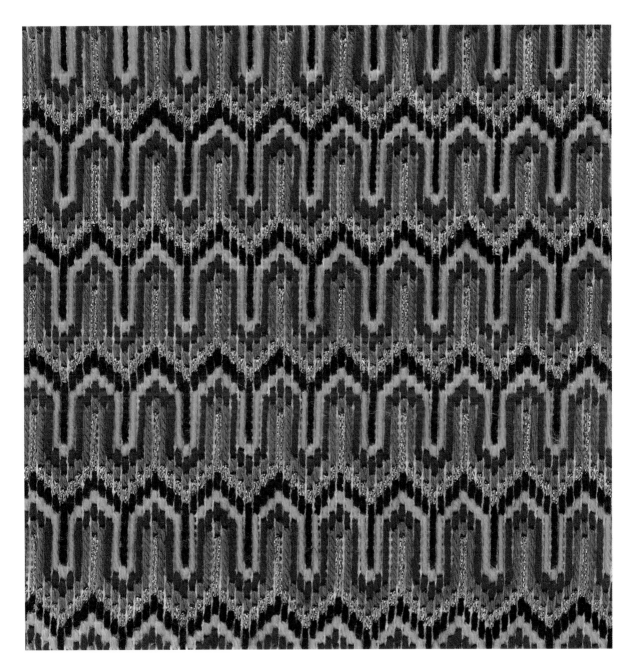

YOU WILL NEED

Yarn 5g (¼oz) per colour, using a mix of acrylics (DK) and gold lurex 2 ply (doubled up to make 4 ply)

Mono canvas (10CT) 22 x 22cm (9 x 9in), leaving a 2cm (¾in) border around the edges

Tapestry needle

- Gold lurex
- Mauve
- Fuchsia
- Sunshine gold
- Purple

This design is inspired by the rich opulent colours associated with Bohemia and the traditional colour of royalty, to reflect the romance of the original bargello story.

BOXED HUNGARIAN POINT

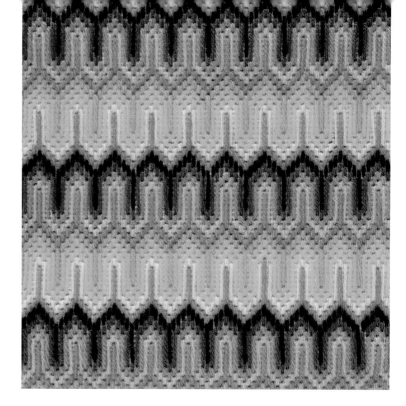

VARIATION 1

YOU WILL NEED

Yarn 5g (¼oz) per colour, using a mix of acrylics (DK)
Mono canvas (10CT) 22 x 22cm (9 x 9in), leaving a 2cm (¾in) border around the edges
Tapestry needle

- Saffron yellow
- Pale lavender
- Mid lavender
- Deep lavender
- Purple
- Light peppermint
- Peppermint
- Deep peppermint
- Heather green

Lavender-blues and lavender-greens. This cool pastel palette is inspired entirely by the beauty and colour diversity of this most fragrant and ubiquitous of herbs.

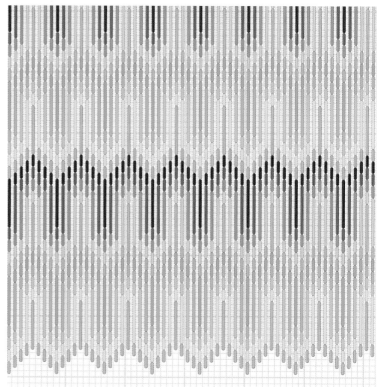

VARIATION 2

YOU WILL NEED
Yarn 5g (¼oz) per colour, using a mix of acrylics (DK)
Mono canvas (10CT) 22 x 22cm (9 x 9in), leaving a 2cm (¾in) border around the edges
Tapestry needle

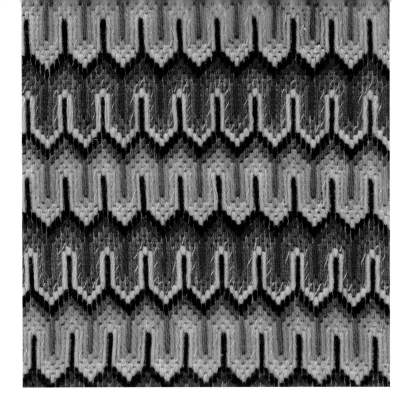

- ● Chocolate
- ○ Pale pink
- ◐ Raspberry with cotton fleck
- ◑ Bubblegum pink
- ● Deep raspberry
- ○ Pineapple
- ◌ Apricot with cotton fleck
- ● Tangy orange
- ● Burnt orange

A traditionally faded bargello in mouthwatering shades of raspberry and tangerine. This zesty number is outlined in vintage chocolate for a nostalgic sepia feel.

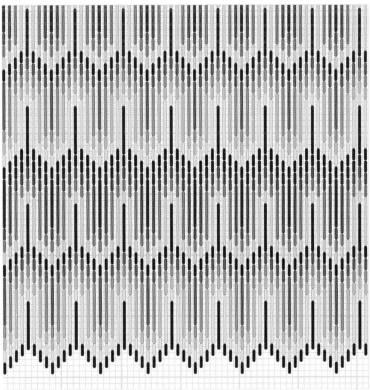

BOXED HUNGARIAN POINT

VARIATION 3

YOU WILL NEED

Yarn 5g (¼oz) per colour, using a mix of acrylics (DK)

Mono canvas (10CT) 22 x 22cm (9 x 9in), leaving a 2cm (¾in) border around the edges

Tapestry needle

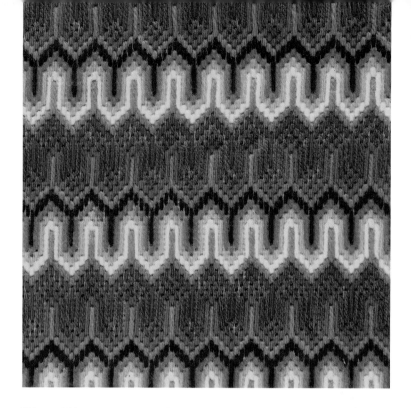

- Mustard
- Neon orange
- Mauve
- Fluorescent purple
- Magenta
- Neon green
- Lemongrass
- Pistachio
- Chestnut

A fiesta of bright vintage colours and clashing neons in an unapologetic celebration of vibrant colour.

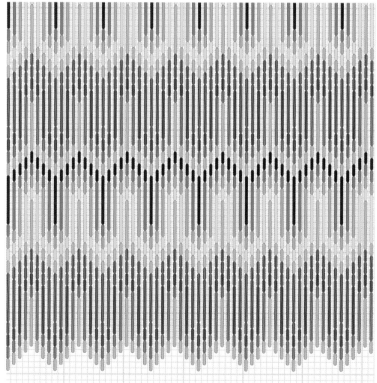

VARIATION 4

YOU WILL NEED

Yarn 5g (⅛oz) per colour, using a mix of acrylics (DK)

Mono canvas (10CT) 22 x 22cm (9 x 9in), leaving a 2cm (¾in) border around the edges

Tapestry needle

- ● Chocolate
- ● Lavender blue
- ● Lavender
- ● Lilac
- ● Pale lilac
- ● Paradise pink
- ● Pink
- ● Blancmange
- ● Baby pink
- ● Coral
- ● Vintage peach
- ● Nude
- ● Perfect peach

- ● Denim
- ● Moody blue
- ● Sky blue
- ● Baby blue
- ● True rose
- ● Scots heather
- ● Pale pink
- Lemon curd
- Pale lemon
- Cream

This design is inspired by the colours of the hydrangea in all its glorious and delicate splendour, from spring through summer, using traditional bargello fading in pinks, blues, peaches, roses, lilacs and lemons.

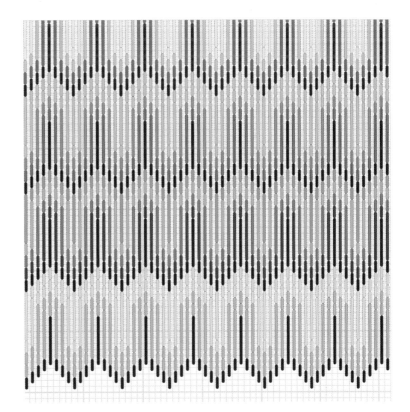

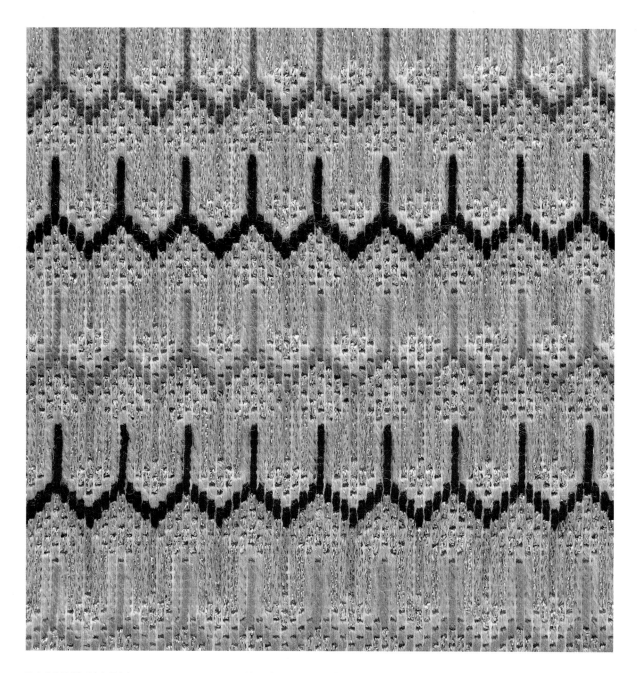

FANCY YARN

Using Boxed Hungarian
Point (see page 84),
this design is a vision
of glittering golds in a
traditional bargello fade,
highlighted with rich hues
of olive and claret.

- Champagne with glitter
- Gold lurex
- Gold with glitter
- Old gold with glitter
- Pea green
- Ruby
- Lemongrass
- Claret
- Olive

BOXED HUNGARIAN POINT

Boxed Hungarian Point is repeated at over four times the featured sample size to create a fabulous framed wall hanging. Mono canvas was used for this project, which demonstrates beautifully how any of the designs can be repeated at a larger scale to great effect.

Featured stitches
Climbing Brick Stitch (see page 16)
Parallel Brick Stitch (see page 17)
Curve Stitch (see page 18)

LOLLIPOPS

Moving from summer to autumn, with beach hues in between, this classic Lollipops sampler could be extended to fill a large canvas or made small enough to fit a garment detail.

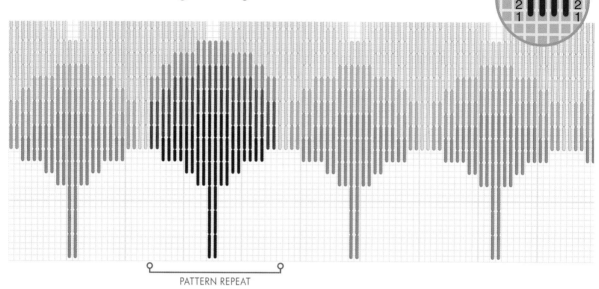

PATTERN REPEAT

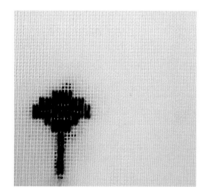

1 Form a base for the lollipop by starting 22 meshes in from the baseline. Three pairs of stitches make up the stem, which is topped with six stitches. Continue to work horizontally in rows across the top as shown on the chart, noting the half stitch of 3 meshes at each side of the second row.

2 Change the colour for each of the next three rows, following the chart.

3 Repeat steps 1 and 2 for each lollipop, working diagonally up the canvas.

YOU WILL NEED

Yarn 5g (¼oz) per colour, using a mix of acrylics (DK)

Mono canvas (10CT) 22 x 22cm (9 x 9in), leaving a 2cm (¾in) border around the edges

Tapestry needle

- Blackberry
- Currant
- Vintage rose
- Rose
- Classic yellow
- Bright lemon
- Primrose
- Pale lemon

- Denim
- Azure
- Sky blue
- Turquoise
- Pear
- Candy green
- Bright green
- Lemongrass

Lollipops is an iconic motif design giving wonderful opportunities to show off that classic bargello fade over four colour stages. This design is particularly effective for showcasing textured yarns.

LOLLIPOPS

VARIATION 1

YOU WILL NEED

Yarn 5g (¼oz) per colour, using a mix of acrylics (DK)
Mono canvas (10CT) 22 x 22cm (9 x 9in), leaving a 2cm (¾in) border around the edges
Tapestry needle

- Mulberry
- Violet
- Grape
- Mauve
- Aquamarine
- Light Prussian blue
- Electric blue
- Azure
- Vintage peach
- Orange
- Terracotta
- Burnt orange

This is a traditional sample in complementary tones of Lollipops, fading from light to dark in shades of orange, blue and purple.

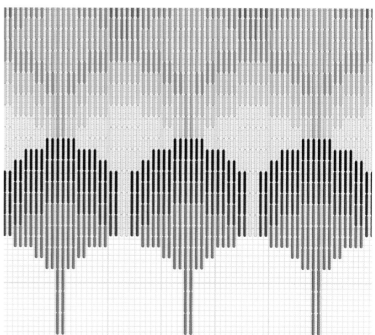

VARIATION 2

YOU WILL NEED

Yarn 20g (1oz) per colour, using a mix of acrylics (DK)

Mono canvas (10CT) 22 x 22cm (9 x 9in), leaving a 2cm (¾in) border around the edges

Tapestry needle

- Mulberry
- Mauve
- Blonde

This sweet shop-inspired mix of purples and warm cream creates a lovely pattern using only three colours. The pattern is exactly the same as the sample on the next page, but with a change in the colour layout.

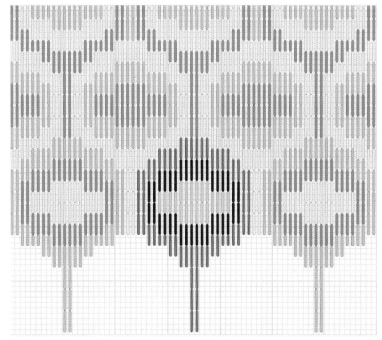

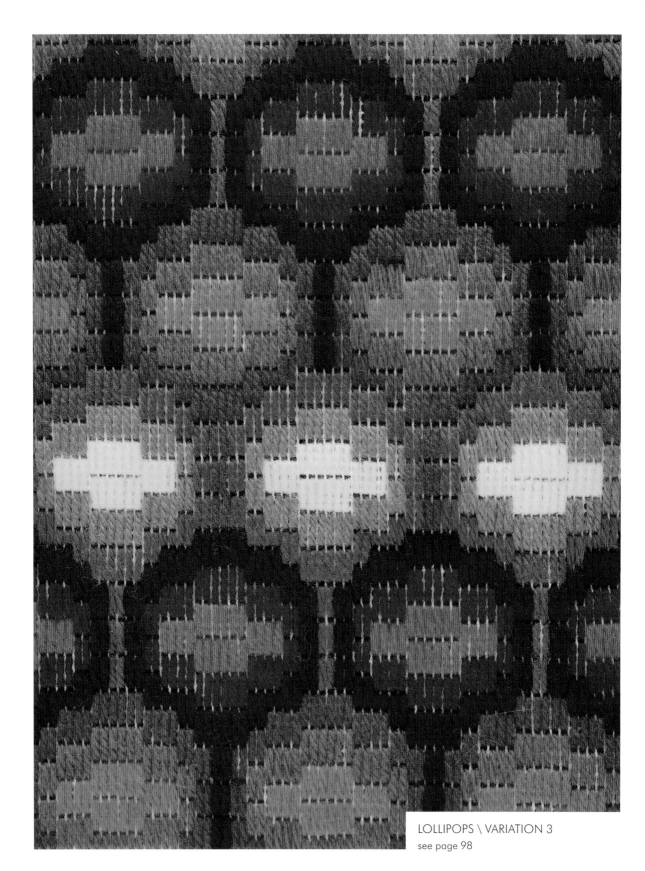

LOLLIPOPS \ VARIATION 3
see page 98

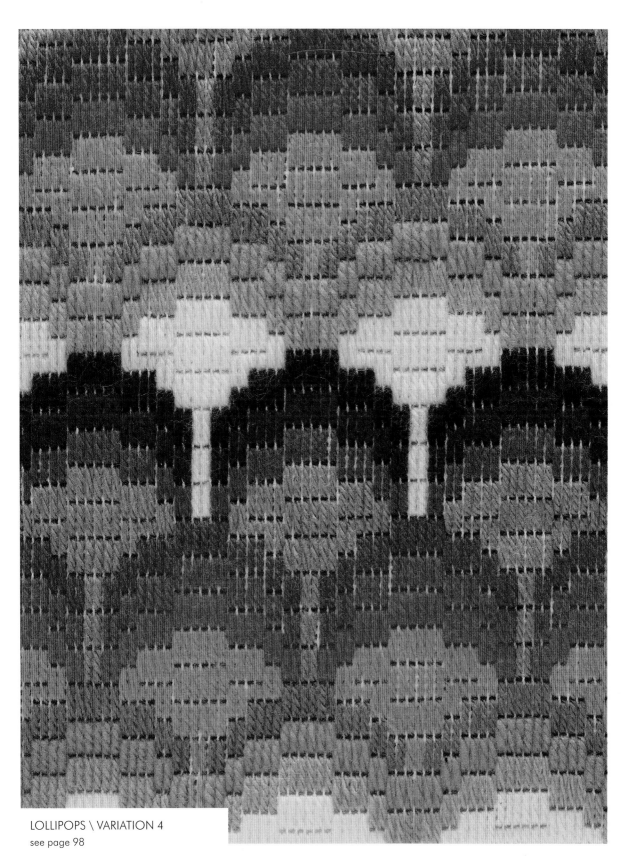

LOLLIPOPS \ VARIATION 4
see page 98

LOLLIPOPS

VARIATION 3
see page 96

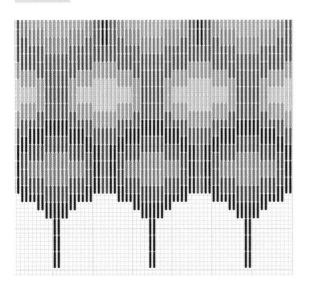

VARIATION 4
see page 97

YOU WILL NEED
Yarn 5g (¼oz) per colour, using a mix of acrylics (DK)
Mono canvas (10CT) 22 x 22cm (9 x 9in), leaving a
2cm (¾in) border around the edges
Tapestry needle

- Claret
- Cherry red
- Bubblegum pink
- Olive
- Light olive
- Neon green
- Fox
- Burnt orange
- Neon orange

Neon centres glow in the midst of
these warm autumnal shades of green,
red and rust.

YOU WILL NEED
Yarn 5g (¼oz) per colour, using a mix of acrylics (DK)
Mono canvas (10CT) 22 x 22cm (9 x 9in), leaving a
2cm (¾in) border around the edges
Tapestry needle

- Fawn
- Sable
- Chocolate
- Darkest brown
- Pale lemon
- Dijon mustard
- Mustard
- Fields of gold
- Pink
- Bubblegum pink
- Magenta
- Deep raspberry

This design combines an array of
fresh pastels with chocolate-brown; a
selection of ice-cream colours to pick
from the dessert menu. It is so pretty
that you could eat it!

FANCY YARN

In this version of the Lollipops design (see page 92), each lollipop is topped with a fluffy line of tinsel wool, alongside complementary shades of DK.

- Yellow green
- Pear
- Pale green tinsel wool
- Mauve
- Fluorescent purple
- Purple/silver tinsel wool
- Orange
- Tangy orange
- Orange tinsel wool

ADVANCED

This chapter is more, more, more! More
complex designs to further your skills, more
colours in each design and more changes
in stitch size to really keep your attention.
Retro is an homage to the 1970s in a series
of beautiful colour fades, Traditional Hungarian
Point is a real skill builder with countless
applications and the grand finale is our
amazing and magical Lanterns.

Featured stitches
Climbing Brick Stitch (see page 16)
Parallel Brick Stitch (see page 17)
Curve Stitch (see page 18)

RETRO

The key to this design is to start with the central oval and then to build an outline for the other ovals. You then fill in the colour bands within the ovals before creating the diamonds in between.

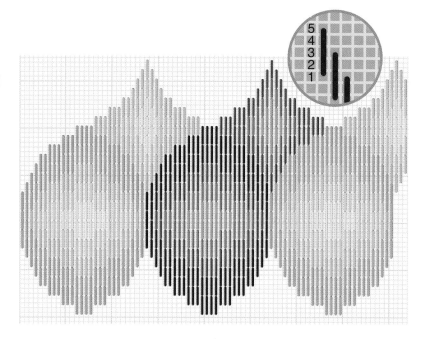

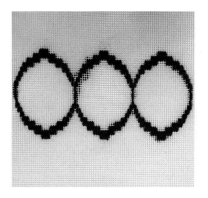

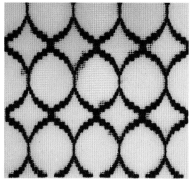

1 Work your first stitch across the centre of the canvas, 14 meshes to the left. Work Curve Stitch to create the top half of the oval, as shown in the chart. Work the bottom half of the oval to return to the starting point. Repeat to create two more ovals.

2 Work the remaining ovals to fill the canvas.

3 To fill in the ovals, use curve stitch in rows, layering the upper and then lower sections.

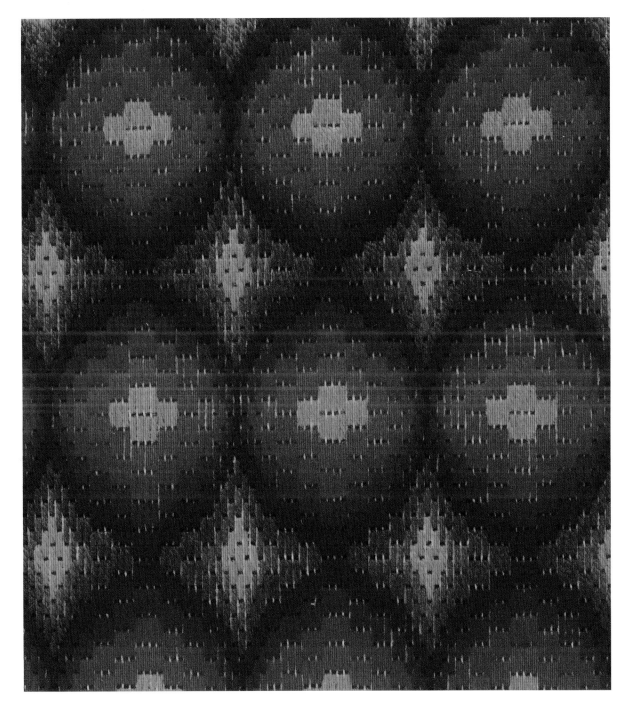

YOU WILL NEED

Yarn 5g (¼oz) per colour, using a mix of acrylics (DK)

Mono canvas (10CT) 22 x 22cm (9 x 9in), leaving a 2cm (¾in) border around the edges

Tapestry needle

- Claret
- Ladybird
- Signal red
- Bubblegum pink
- Pink
- Dusky pink
- Vintage rose

Moody jewel shades meet dusky pinks in this dark, retro-inspired design.

RETRO

VARIATION 1

YOU WILL NEED
Yarn 5g (¼oz) per colour, using a mix of acrylics (DK)
Mono canvas (10CT) 22 x 22cm (9 x 9in), leaving a 2cm (¾in) border around the edges
Tapestry needle

- ● Dark olive
- ● Army green
- ● Olive
- ● Deep chartreuse
- ● Pea green
- ● Pistachio
- ● Gold lurex

This piece brings an authentic Mediterranean vibe, using a full range of olive tones.

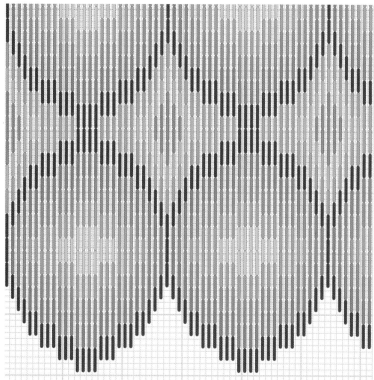

VARIATION 2

YOU WILL NEED

Yarn 5g (¼oz) per colour, using a mix of acrylics (DK)

Mono canvas (10CT) 22 x 22cm (9 x 9in), leaving a 2cm (¾in) border around the edges

Tapestry needle

- ● Rust
- ● Fox
- ● Burnt orange
- ● Yam
- ● Orange
- ● Tangy orange
- ● Neon orange

Layers of orange meet foxy tones as these glorious sunsets light a burning bargello sky.

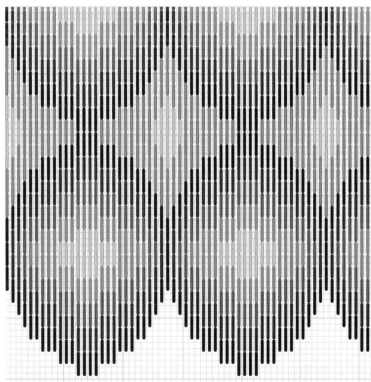

RETRO \ VARIATION 3
see page 108

RETRO \ VARIATION 4
see page 108

RETRO

VARIATION 3
see page 106

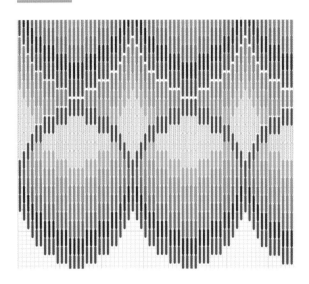

VARIATION 4
see page 107

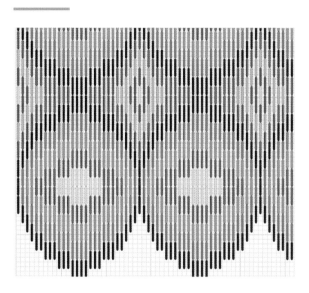

YOU WILL NEED
Yarn 5g (¼oz) per colour, using a mix of acrylics (DK)
Mono canvas (10CT) 22 x 22cm (9 x 9in), leaving a 2cm (¾in)
border around the edges
Tapestry needle

- Iced gem with glitter
- Baby blue
- Pale blue
- Ice blue with glitter
- Sky blue
- Airforce blue
- Denim
- Admiral grey

The sophisticated ice-blue
palette cools down this sample.

YOU WILL NEED
Yarn 5g (¼oz) per colour, using a mix of acrylics (DK)
Mono canvas (10CT) 22 x 22cm (9 x 9in), leaving a 2cm (¾in)
border around the edges
Tapestry needle

- Fuchsia
- Teal
- Yam
- Magenta
- Cream
- Bubblegum pink
- Sky blue
- Royal blue

The multicoloured palette for
this delightfully bright design
uses all of the happiest shades
of the colour spectrum. A
pattern to make you smile.

RETRO

This modern throw cushion glows with vintage vibes. The Retro design in a contemporary bright palette works everywhere, from sunroom to bedroom.

Featured stitches
Climbing Brick Stitch (see page 16)
Parallel Brick Stitch (see page 17)
Hungarian Stitch (see pages 22–23)

TRADITIONAL HUNGARIAN POINT

This is the original design from the Bargello Museum in Florence. The forked design can be worked in four or eight colours, and it can be used for large or small designs as the stitch is not long enough to warp. The key to this design is to establish a foundation row (the teal row in this example). The rest of the pattern is formed by sewing around the foundation row in Hungarian Stitch.

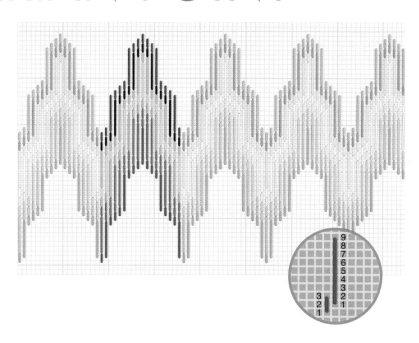

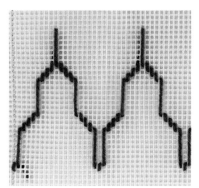

1 Starting from the left-hand edge of the canvas, stitch the foundation row in teal yarn, using stitches over 3 meshes and 9 meshes, as shown in the chart.

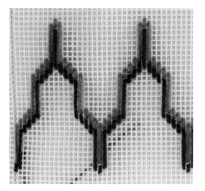

2 Working directly above the foundation row, follow the chart for the second row in deep lime.

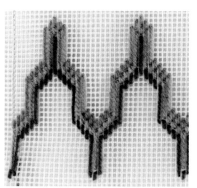

3 Change to mid-mauve yarn and complete the third row. Use pale mauve for the fourth row. Repeat steps 1–3 with the next four yarn colours. You have now completed one colour repeat. Continue in this way to complete the design.

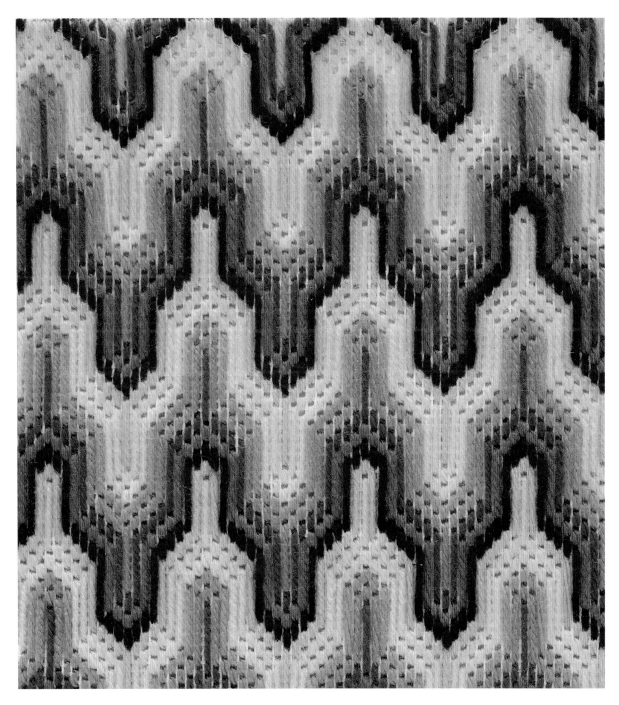

YOU WILL NEED

Yarn 5g (¼oz) per colour, using a mix of acrylics (DK)

Mono canvas (10CT) 22 x 22cm (9 x 9in), leaving a 2cm (¾in) border around the edges

Tapestry needle

- ● Teal
- ● Deep lime
- ● Mid mauve
- ● Pale mauve
- ● Mint

- ○ Lime
- ● Blackberry
- ● Fluorescent purple

In colours reminiscent of an English country garden, this cool palette showcases tones of blackberry, teal and lime, which are then mirrored in their own pastel hues for the repeat row.

TRADITIONAL HUNGARIAN POINT

VARIATION 1

YOU WILL NEED

Yarn 5g (¼oz) per colour, using a mix of acrylics (DK)

Mono canvas (10CT) 22 x 22cm (9 x 9in), leaving a 2cm (¾in) border around the edges

Tapestry needle

- Classic yellow
- Sunshine gold
- Mustard
- Magenta
- Fluorescent purple
- Mauve
- Rust
- Neon orange

A joyous kaleidoscope of happy sunshine yellows, berry shades and vibrant neons. You will smile as you sew this one!

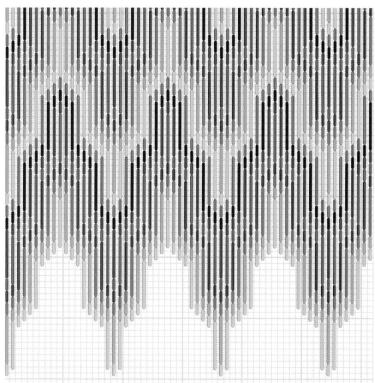

VARIATION 2

YOU WILL NEED

Yarn 5g (¼oz) per colour, using a mix of acrylics (DK)

Mono canvas (10CT) 22 x 22cm (9 x 9in), leaving a 2cm (¾in) border around the edges

Tapestry needle

- Mustard
- Cherry red
- Ladybird
- Signal red

A bold but simple working of Hungarian Point in just four colours, three of which are red tones. This design demonstrates that sometimes less really is more. The yellow brings definition to balance out the accents of red.

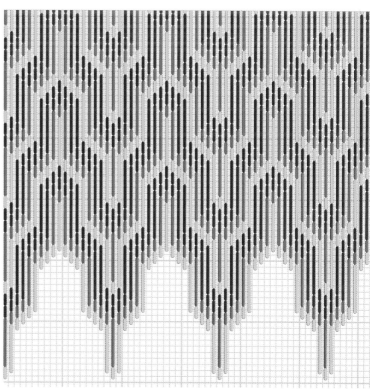

TRADITIONAL HUNGARIAN POINT \ VARIATION 3
see page 116

TRADITIONAL HUNGARIAN POINT \ VARIATION 4
see page 116

TRADITIONAL HUNGARIAN POINT

VARIATION 3
see page 114

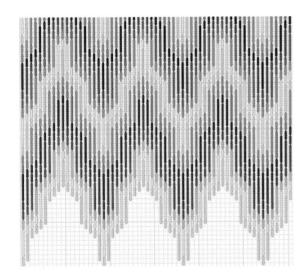

VARIATION 4
see page 115

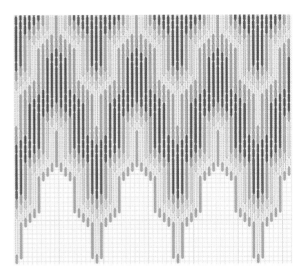

YOU WILL NEED
Yarn 5g (⅕oz) per colour, using a mix of acrylics (DK) and gold lurex 2 ply (doubled up to make 4 ply)
Mono canvas (10CT) 22 x 22cm (9 x 9in), leaving a 2cm (¾in) border around the edges
Tapestry needle

- Rose
- Paradise pink
- Raspberry
- Mulberry
- Burnt gold
- Gold lurex
- Champagne with glitter
- Cream
- Mauve
- Fluorescent purple
- Heather
- Darkest purple

NOTE: On this design, the long stitch is made from mesh 1 to mesh 7 with 5 meshes in the middle. Short stitches are as before.

A romantic interpretation inspired by rococo interiors, featuring soft pinks and mauves complemented by cream and gold for a soft but opulent feel.

YOU WILL NEED
Yarn 5g (⅕oz) per colour, using a mix of acrylics (DK) and silver lurex 2 ply (doubled up to make 4 ply)
Mono canvas (10CT) 22 x 22cm (9 x 9in), leaving a 2cm (¾in) border around the edges
Tapestry needle

- Silver lurex
- Cream
- Oyster
- Sand
- Rose with glitter
- Violet with glitter
- Light heather
- Grey mauve

This design is a moodier take on the rococo theme. Gold and marble colours against palatial purples bring a lavish look to this interpretation.

TRADITIONAL HUNGARIAN POINT

A gorgeous on-trend shoulder bag bringing traditional Hungarian Point into the modern age. This bright fiery palette will work with any outfit too! Use duo canvas for this project to give the bag better movement and strength.

Featured stitches
Climbing Brick Stitch (see page 16)
Parallel Brick Stitch (see page 17)
Hungarian Stitch (see pages 22–23)

LANTERNS

Here are some magic lanterns to light up your bargello world. This beautiful and complex design combines your Hungarian Stitch skills with your ability to make a frame – then you get to colour it in. It can be worked in fades, stripes or both – and there's nothing like putting some sparkle in your Lanterns to make them really shine.

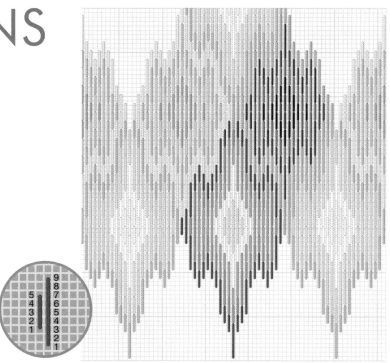

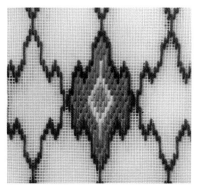

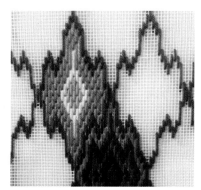

1 Create a diamond shape in the centre of the canvas using Climbing Brick Stitch, as shown on the chart. Change colour and surround the shape with a single long stitch at the top and bottom, and fill in the rest with brick stitch. Change colour again, and follow the edge of the diamond, creating wing shapes at each side and joining with a single stitch.

2 Follow the same process, following stitches around the outside for the next two cycles, finishing on the fifth colour. Continue with the fifth colour to create outlines of each lantern over the whole canvas, making a framework.

3 Working this time from the outside towards the inside, stitch the second lantern shape in the same way as the first, following the chart for guidance.

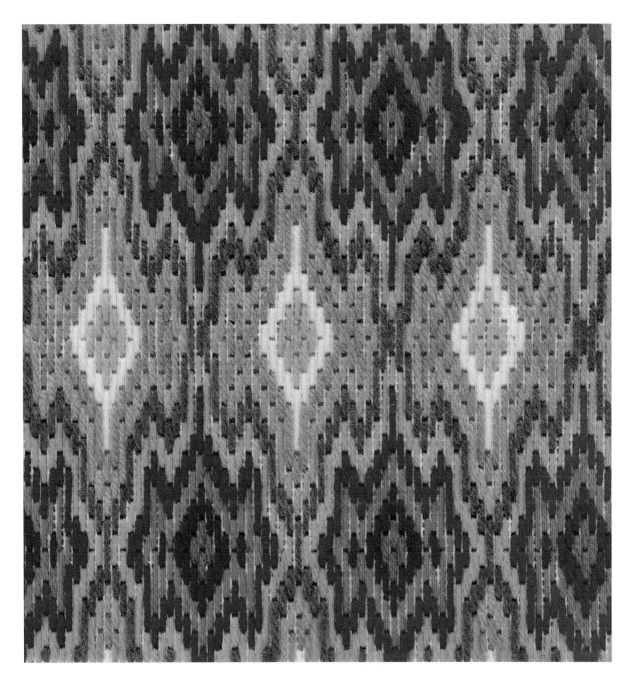

YOU WILL NEED

Yarn 5g (¼oz) per colour, using a mix of acrylics (DK)

Mono canvas (10CT) 22 x 22cm (9 x 9in), leaving a 2cm (¾in) border around the edges

Tapestry needle

- Chartreuse
- Primrose
- Lemongrass
- Fields of gold
- Orchard
- Vintage peach
- Signal red
- Tangerine
- Ladybird
- Burnt orange

A William Morris-inspired Lanterns design in natural but bold tones clearly demonstrates the sophistication of this particular pattern.

LANTERNS

VARIATION 1

YOU WILL NEED

Yarn 5g (¼oz) per colour, using a
mix of acrylics (DK)
Mono canvas (10CT) 22 x 22cm
(9 x 9in), leaving a 2cm (¾in) border
around the edges
Tapestry needle

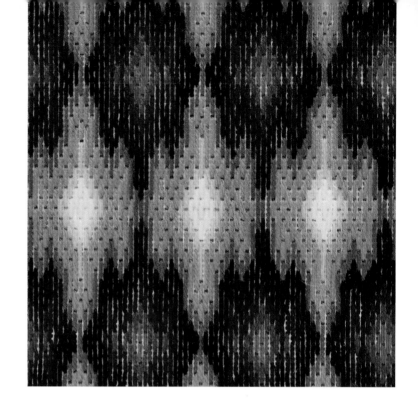

- Neon yellow
- Lime green
- Golden olive
- Pea green
- Olive
- Dark burgundy
- Claret
- Burgundy
- Raspberry
- Magenta

With rich plummy hues against an
array of Mediterranean greens, this
is a true bargello fade. Both Lanterns
fade dark to light from the outside to
make for a moodier tone, and are lit
by striking neon centres that set this
sample aglow.

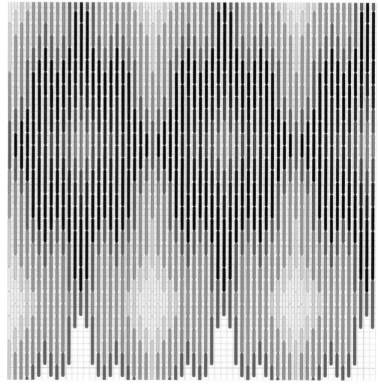

VARIATION 2

YOU WILL NEED

Yarn 5g (¼oz) per colour, using a
mix of acrylics (DK)
Mono canvas (10CT) 22 x 22cm
(9 x 9in), leaving a 2cm (¾in) border
around the edges
Tapestry needle

- Cream
- Bright Lemon
- Saffron
- Apricot with cotton fleck
- Mustard
- Baby pink
- Pink
- Rose
- Raspberry with cotton fleck
- Raspberry

A summery version of Lanterns with
tasty tones of tangerine and ripe
raspberry. Interest is added to the
texture using the white cotton-flecked
acrylic in one line of each Lantern.

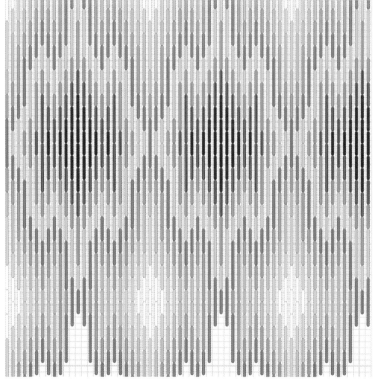

LANTERNS

VARIATION 3

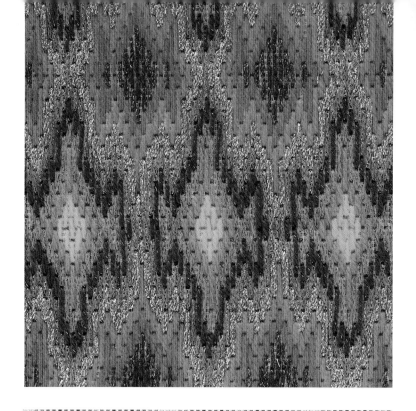

YOU WILL NEED

Yarn 5g (¼oz) per colour, using a mix of acrylics (DK) and gold lurex 2 ply (doubled up to make 4 ply)

Mono canvas (10CT) 22 x 22cm (9 x 9in), leaving a 2cm (¾in) border around the edges

Tapestry needle

- Turquoise
- Azure
- Jade with glitter
- Teal with glitter
- Old gold with glitter
- Silver lurex
- Neon orange
- Tangy orange
- Metallic orange
- Burnt orange with glitter

A bawdy celebration of peacock-feather blues and oranges against a heady and glamorous 1970s silver and gold backdrop.

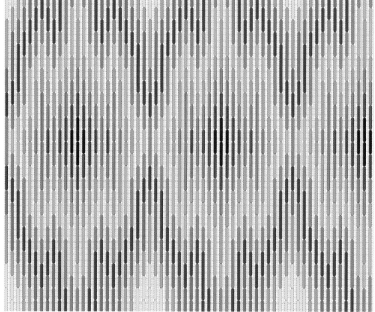

VARIATION 4

YOU WILL NEED

Yarn 5g (¼oz) per colour, using a mix of acrylics (DK)

Mono canvas (10CT) 22 x 22cm (9 x 9in), leaving a 2cm (¾in) border around the edges

Tapestry needle

- Baby blue
- Nude with glitter
- Denim
- Cherry pie
- Moody blue
- Baby pink
- Forget-me-not
- Pink
- Iced gem with glitter
- Forest fruit

This Lanterns design uses a striped variant of the main pattern in mirrored colour tones.

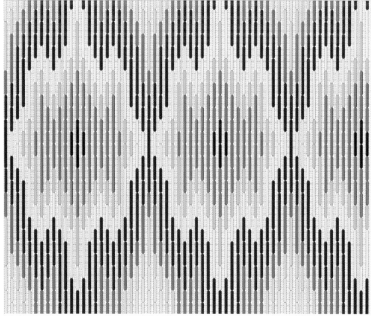

FANCY YARN

An über-glamorous Lanterns design (see page 118) in cool Art Deco colours made entirely of metallic and glitter yarns. Think Tiffany lamp in bargello!

- Metallic optic white
- Metallic turquoise
- Metallic yellow
- Metallic optic jade
- Jade with glitter
- Old gold with glitter
- Turquoise with glitter
- Fuchsia with glitter
- Metallic pink
- Metallic gold

LANTERNS

This is a glorious way to show off the Lanterns design in your sunroom. With its natural Tuscan tones, this upholstery cushion just sings with style. Made using duo canvas for strength and flexibility, this cushion is made up of four edge bands and one large piece of bargello work (the back is optional).

TAKING BARGELLO FURTHER

Now you have the designs, it's time to use them.
In Edges and Borders, learn various spiral band
techniques, along with chains and staggered
stripes. The Textural and Canvas Work pieces
will inspire you to combine bargello ideas
with other stitching disciplines. In Freestyling,
learn that there is so much you now know and
can take forward to create your own unique
bespoke projects.

SPIRAL BANDS

Spiral Bands are a staple of bargello edging work.
Introduced here in their simplest form, they are as versatile
as they are striking.

The sweep of the curve is created using single stitches for depth and Parallel
Brick Stitch for breadth – for this reason, it can be adapted to suit any size of
border space you wish to fill.

Originally, the design tended to be used for bell pulls and drapes – however,
in modern bargello, it can be used to frame a wall hanging, edge a lampshade
or cushion, or make a simple birthday card. It is also an excellent design to
work if you would like to practise Curve Stitch.

Start from the bottom left-hand corner with a series of single stitches, then
increase to pairs and multiples, always ensuring that you mirror these from the
centre stitches.

Featured stitches
Climbing Brick Stitch (see page 16)
Parallel Brick Stitch (see page 17)
Curve Stitch (see page 18)
Scottish Stitch (see page 19)

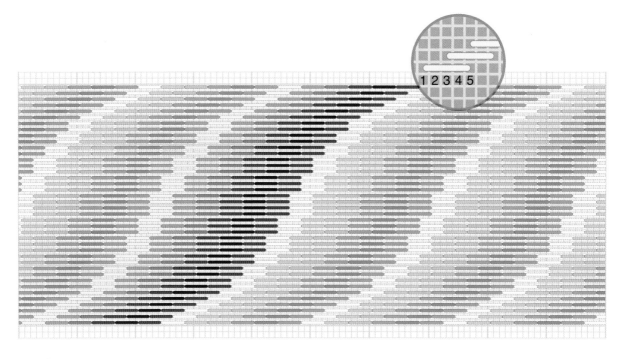

<table>
<tr><td>⬤ Bright lemon</td><td>⬤ Forest fruit</td></tr>
<tr><td>⬤ Fields of gold</td><td>◯ White</td></tr>
<tr><td>⬤ Burnt orange</td><td>⬤ Steel grey</td></tr>
<tr><td>⬤ Ladybird</td><td>⬤ Black</td></tr>
<tr><td>⬤ Claret</td><td></td></tr>
</table>

In these examples, we have used a fade of autumn colours, from claret to bright lemon, to create soft curves and a monochrome palette, which gives a harder and more defined finish and creates an optical illusion.

CROSSED SPIRAL BANDS

Crossed Spiral Bands are worked using only four bands of colour and – like Spiral Bands (see page 128) – are flexible enough to work over narrow and broader border spaces.

As you can see in this example, the depth of the border will significantly affect how circular or oval the central shape is; this is achieved by varying the number of stitches set in your first line.

Starting from the bottom left-hand corner, work the full width of the border, then work back from your centre stitches to keep the design on track. This design varies from Spiral Bands in that it relies on a heavy use of parallel rather than single stitches to work, so please bear this in mind when adapting it to fit.

Featured stitches
Climbing Brick Stitch (see page 16)
Parallel Brick Stitch (see page 17)
Curve Stitch (see page 18)
Scottish Stitch (see page 19)

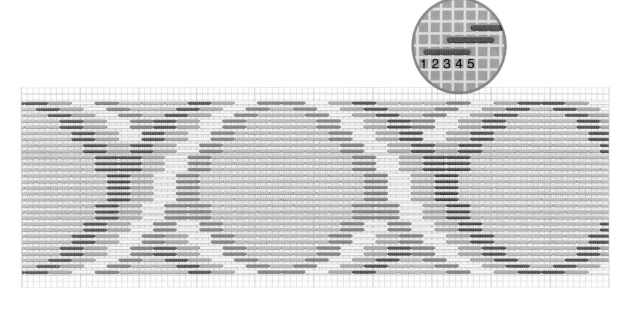

- ● Raspberry
- ● Jade
- ▦ Primrose
- ● Lavender

- ○ Baby blue
- ▦ Baby pink

Using more than four colours will not work on this border as you will lose the shape. We have chosen a pastel palette for these Crossed Spiral Bands; however, they look equally stunning in faded bargello tones or bolder colours.

DIAGONAL STRIPES

Diagonal Stripes produce a simple but effective design – as well as working as a border, they can also be used as a filler or a main design.

The basis of this design is the Climbing Brick Stitch, worked in pairs. The number of stitches can be varied, but there must be an equal number in each step or the diagonal slant cannot be achieved. The stitch size can also be varied, but the rule of thumb is that the stitches must run over an odd number of meshes (eg 1–3, 1–5 or 1–7), as the next stitch is started from the centre point of the last pair.

Featured stitches
Climbing Brick Stitch (see page 16)
Parallel Brick Stitch (see page 17)
Leaf Stitch (see page 20)

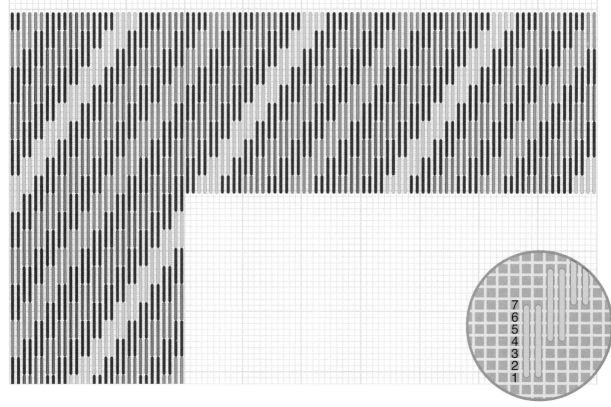

- Chocolate
- Neon orange
- Neon pink
- Neon green
- Coral

In terms of colourways, you can really go for it creatively with this design. We have used a basic stripe with alternating neon colours, but you could also use two colours or an unlimited number, making either defined striping or a full rainbow of bargello fade.

CHAINS

Chains is a classical border that has been used for cushions, drapery and upholstery over centuries of needlework.

This is a fixed design and doesn't translate to changes of size; the maths is so tight that it is only possible to adjust the background stitching (fields of gold in this example) by extending the stitches to fit your border size, so be sure to measure first.

Most of the diagonal stitches are over 7 meshes, but the corners and joints use smaller tailored stitches (3 to 7 meshes) to fit around the intersecting band. In the centre of the chain link is a vertical Scottish Stitch, which can be in a complementary colour or the same as the background stitching. The background stitches are a basic filler stitch and should be worked last.

The corners are the trickiest part of this border; for this reason, we have shown two ways of handling them. In the outer layer, we sewed straight across into the next band, and in the inner layer we have sewn exactly to the diagonal line.

Featured stitches
Climbing Brick Stitch (see page 16)
Parallel Brick Stitch (see page 17)
Scottish Stitch (see page 19)
Leaf Stitch (see page 20)

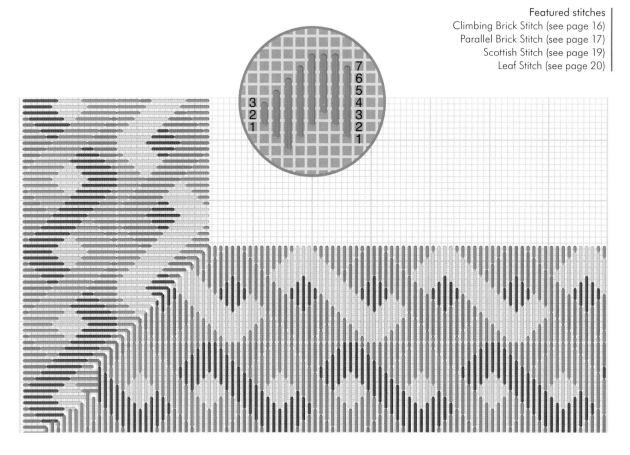

- Azure
- Burnt orange with glitter
- Pale lemon
- Fields of gold

The colourway for this sample is inspired by the art of the Incas, using colours from nature but amplified.

FUSED SPIRAL BANDS

This is by far the most advanced of the Spiral Bands designs, but is visually one of the most rewarding.

Once again, the design can be stretched or minimised to fit your border space by adjusting the numbers of stitches, but the number of colours and bands cannot be adjusted.

On these examples you can see that we have also varied the stitch size. To compact the spiral into a tighter shape, we have worked over only 3 meshes. Similarly, you can use larger sections of stitches over a wider canvas to create a tight spiral.

As with all Spiral Bands designs, start at the bottom left-hand corner of the canvas and work your first line across the width of the border. Work the rest of the design, following the chart and omitting one section of stitches (either one stitch or a series of parallel ones) from the end of each band to make room for the next series of bands.

Featured stitches
Climbing Brick Stitch (see page 16)
Parallel Brick Stitch (see page 17)
Curve Stitch (see page 18)
Scottish Stitch (see page 19)

1 2 3

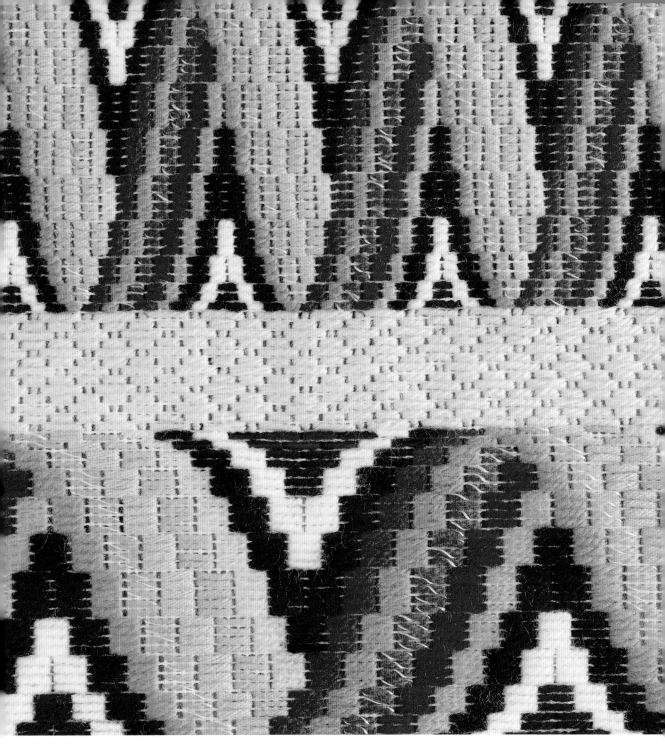

- ● Mustard
- ● Apricot with cotton fleck
- ● Soft gold
- ● Mango
- ● Nude
- ● Burgundy
- Cream

- ● True red
- ● Raspberry
- ● Rose
- ● Raspberry with cotton fleck
- ● Fuchsia
- ● Pink

In this sample, we have opted for a colourway of summer-fruit shades and used a bargello fade to highlight the flow of the spiral.

CLIMBING BRICK STITCH

This is the simplest of stitches, often used for filling in backgrounds, but this design also works well as a beginner sampler if you are trying bargello for the first time.

Formerly known as Gobelin filling stitch, but referred to throughout the book as Climbing Brick Stitch, this works vertically and climbs up and down the canvas.

Using shades of green from pale aqua to olive, we have created a central fade where the colour meets in the middle of the sampler. The trick is entirely in the subtlety of the shading in this piece. Two rows form the central line and two rows of each colour are layered above and below it. Reading from light to dark, then dark to light, makes for a dramatic landscape that could work in any number of projects, as the stitches are both small and even. For more detailed sewing instructions, see Climbing Brick Stitch, on page 16.

Featured stitches
Climbing Brick Stitch (see page 16)
Parallel Brick Stitch (see page 17)

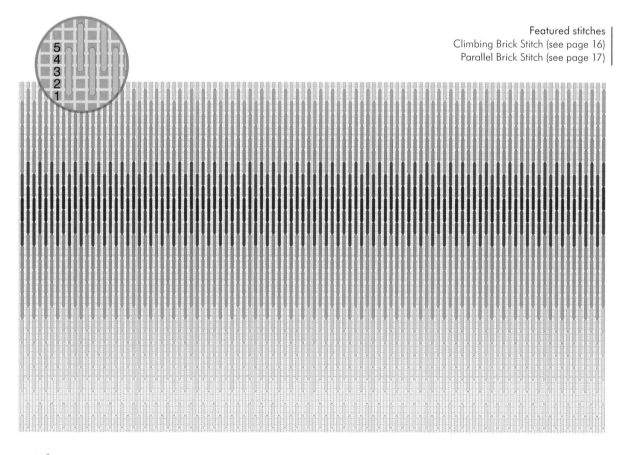

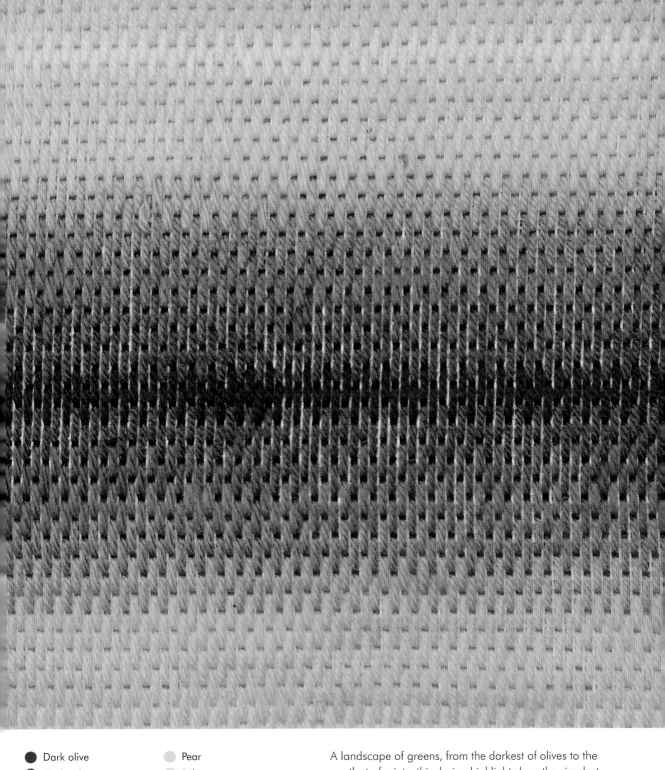

- ● Dark olive
- ● Orchard
- ● Olive
- ● Scouting green
- ● Seaweed
- ● Lime green
- ● Pear
- ● Pale green
- ● Mint
- ● Pale aqua

A landscape of greens, from the darkest of olives to the gentlest of mints, this design highlights how the simplest stitches become glorious with colour.

LEAF STITCH

This is a lovely structural stitch that offers great rewards with its depth and texture. It is sometimes used as a background to suggest foliage or feathers, but is showcased here to demonstrate how it works beautifully as a stand-alone.

You can start from anywhere on the left-hand side of the canvas and work across. Measure out the box for your first stitch (10 meshes up by 7 meshes across) and work each leaf so that its sides are touching the previous leaf (the row of three diagonal stitches). On the next line above, you will work in the gaps between the tips of the leaves. The chart below details how to do this. For more detailed sewing instructions, see Leaf Stitch, on page 20.

Featured stitches
Climbing Brick Stitch (see page 16)
Parallel Brick Stitch (see page 17)
Leaf Stitch (see page 20)

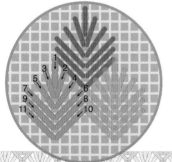

- Fields of gold
- Dusky rose
- Yellow green
- Forest fruit

This colour scheme is made up of four funky colours that refresh this classic stitch with a modern palette of yellow green and dusky rose with rich autumn shades of claret and gold.

DOUBLE CROSS STITCH

The Double Cross Stitch is easy to do and has a lovely tactile feel that creates a sturdy piece of needlework.

It is ideal for making into a cushion or wall hanging, but translates to even larger projects, such as upholstery, as this small stitch lends strength to the work. It can also be relied upon as a filler stitch. The stitch is formed by working a simple cross stitch and then coming back over it diagonally with another smaller cross to make an eight-point star. Repeat throughout. It is that simple.

This stitch patterns very easily and could be made in two colours or using a colour fade (as in this sample). We have created a geometric fade by sewing squares of twenty-five stitches in diagonal rows of eight tones of blue, from ocean blue to midnight. You can, of course, play with this pattern, perhaps changing the size of the squares or using a different tessellating shape.

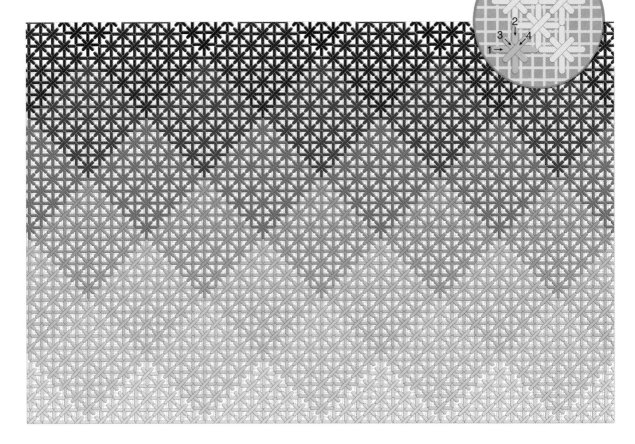

- Midnight
- Indian ink
- Sapphire
- Denim
- Azure
- Sky blue
- Turquoise
- Light Prussian blue
- Ocean blue

Moody blues create a chequerboard sky in this sensational double cross stitch.

PYRAMIDS

Using only the humble cross stitch and a graduating geometric line, this is a striking piece that celebrates bargello without actually using any!

Rather than Florentine/Hungarian bargello, in this design we were inspired by the long-standing American tradition of bargello quilting and its astounding use of geometric colour fades.

Working across the canvas, start in the centre with a row of three cross stitches, and build in blocks of four crosses up and three across to make the bricks that create this staggered pyramid. To replicate the bargello shading, we start in shades of lilac that build up over seven colours to become deep purples.

This technique gives a nod to bargello, and cross stitch is a handy addition to your needlework skills that can be used on its own or mixed in with bargello designs. Don't be afraid to experiment and see where it takes you.

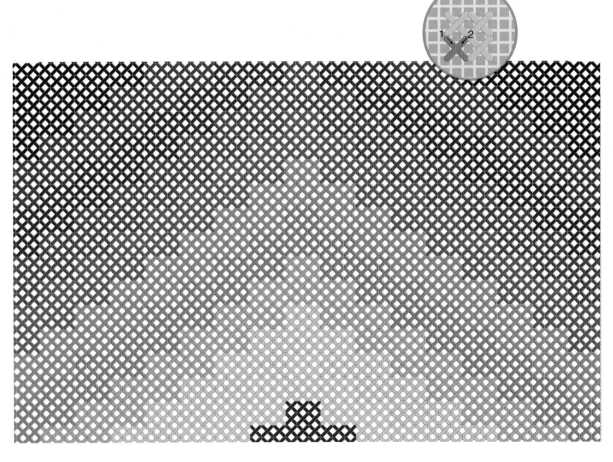

- ● Darkest purple
- ● Grey lilac
- ● Lilac
- ● Scots heather
- ● Fluorescent purple
- ● Lavender
- ● Purple steel
- ● Purple
- ● Revolution
- ● Indigo
- ● Pansy
- ● Royal purple

From the petals of the pansy to delicate heather, the purples of nature meet precision geometry in this purple powerhouse.

HEXAGONS

Often overlooked as a filler, Scottish Stitch makes for a smooth tactile finish while giving the impression of a quilted surface.

To create this diagonal version of the Scottish Stitch (the vertical version is explained on page 19), you need to work on a 5 x 5 square of meshes and sew diagonally. First, make a 3-mesh stitch over the top left-hand corner, then a 4-mesh stitch alongside, followed by a 5-mesh stitch from corner to corner. Another 4-mesh and 3-mesh stitch in parallel completes the square. The graduating pattern is distinctive, so, if you check your work often, any mistakes can be spotted and rectified quickly.

Featured stitches
Climbing Brick Stitch (see page 16)
Parallel Brick Stitch (see page 17)
Scottish Stitch (see page 19)

- Pale peach
- Peach
- Tangerine
- Orange
- Neon orange
- Vintage peach
- Tan
- Fox
- Rust

To give a warm and romantic feel, here we use nine tones in an orange spectrum, from nude to tan, fading diagonally down the canvas.

BLAZING BAUBLES

This is an original design employing techniques from Pomegranates (see page 68) and Lanterns (see page 118).

The place to start with Blazing Baubles is by setting the framework at the outer rim of the lemon and diamond shapes. From there, keep working in circles from the outside edges inwards. Work either clockwise or anticlockwise only, depending on your preference.

The diamonds are mostly brick-stitched and should begin at the darkest purple, again working from the outside towards the centres.

As this design features smaller, uniform stitches and is repetitive, it is versatile enough to be used on upholstery, cushions, accessories or wall hangings.

The colours can be adapted and the design would work with changes in textures and yarns, but will not work in stripes or alternating colours because definition would be lost.

- Scots heather
- Mustard
- Sunshine yellow
- Classic yellow
- Lemon
- Pale lemon
- Revolution
- Fluorescent purple

For this version of Blazing Baubles we have used a modern
palette of mauves and lemons worked in a bargello fade.

Featured stitches
Climbing Brick Stitch (see page 16)
Parallel Brick Stitch (see page 17)
Hungarian Stitch (see pages 22–23)

REFLECTED HUNGARIAN POINT MOTIF

The Hungarian Point Motif is a staple of traditional bargello work and has been featured throughout the centuries in numerous furnishings and wall hangings.

Start from the left-hand side of the canvas with the lowest row of the upper motif (the reds) and then work the upper rows to where it meets the lower motif (the greens). Mirror the upper work to create the lower motif. To check your work, you should have a working rhythm of two long stitches followed by four small ones. Work the Hungarian Point until both motifs are established. For more detailed sewing instructions, see Hungarian Stitch on pages 22–23.

The background may look complex at first; however, the trick is to follow the long stitches in a diagonal line on either side of the motifs, then do the same with the smaller ones. When the zigzag stage is done, you can complete the piece by filling in with Climbing Brick Stitch.

You can mix things up with the motif colours to change the palette, but we recommend that the background is all the same colour or tones of one colour.

- ● Claret
- ● Cherry red
- ● Ladybird
- ● Signal red
- ● Olive
- ● Lemongrass

- ● Pea green
- ● Lime
- ● Neon yellow
- ● Gold lurex
- ● Champagne with glitter

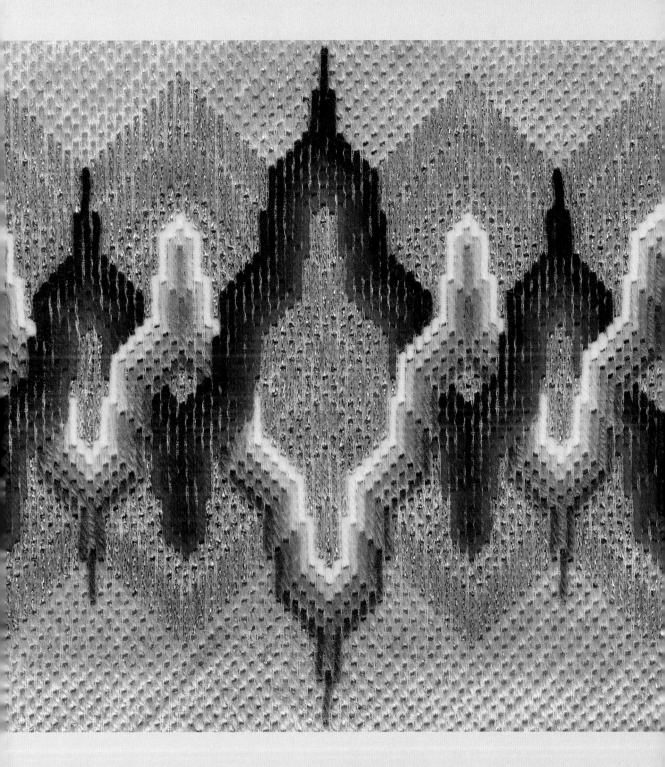

Gold and champagne colours provide a glittering backdrop to this dramatic and complex Hungarian Point Motif of rich, Italian-inspired hues.

Featured stitches
Climbing Brick Stitch (see page 16)
Parallel Brick Stitch (see page 17)
Curve Stitch (see page 18)

LOZENGES

This design is a great example of how you can really freestyle with bargello and use elements of different designs and stitches all in one piece.

To start this design, you first need to draw the lozenge shapes on your mono canvas. The lozenge on the left has been worked using a style adapted from Lollipops (see page 92). Start by setting in the design across the centre of the lozenge and then work both upwards and downwards to complete. The second lozenge is a reworking of Basket Weave (see page 76), but with Parallel Brick Stitch in pairs at the centre instead of a cross.

 The background is a simple Climbing Brick Stitch, cleverly worked in a bargello fade of oceanic blues to make the lozenges look as if they are floating in the sea. This design is easily adapted, so you can fill in the lozenges with whichever patterns from the book appeal to you.

- Fluorescent purple
- Candy floss
- Fuchsia
- Forest fruit
- Rose

- Dark vintage rose
- Bubblegum pink
- Background in 11 shades of turquoise

Bold pinks and purples layer and intertwine against a soft, fading aqua sea.

Featured stitches
Climbing Brick Stitch (see page 16)
Parallel Brick Stitch (see page 17)
Curve Stitch (see page 18)

HONEYCOMBS

This design plays with and creates texture by placing the same repeated shape against itself but finished in a completely different way.

You should start by establishing the framework (in coral) which, in this case, are the hexagonal honeycomb cells. These are created in a similar way to Pomegranates (see page 68) and take their technique from Curve Stitch, despite becoming angular in shape!

The coral and yellow honeycomb cells feature a diagonally latticed Climbing Brick Stitch in coral accented with yellow crosses. The striped honeycomb cells are made up of a series of concentric hexagons, using the Curve Stitch and moving inwards to the centre.

This design can be adapted to many bargello styles once the honeycomb cells have been established. You can mix and match them using opposing or complementary patterns, which only adds to the textural richness of the design. There is no limit to the number of patterns you can use in your hexagons; we have used two here, but you could do every cell differently if you wish.

- Coral
- Neon yellow
- Denim
- Paradise pink
- Electric blue

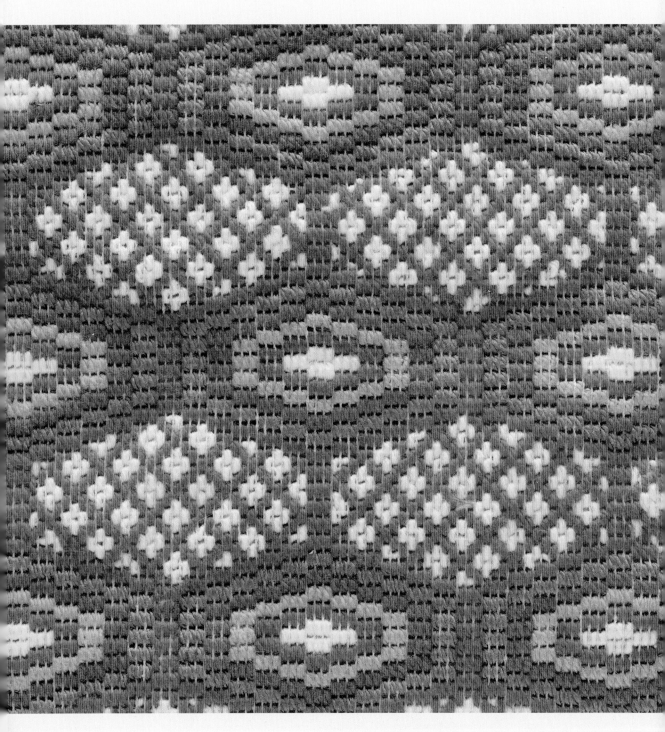

Coral and neon yellow zing these honeycombs to life against beautiful twilight shades.

INDEX

Designs, stitches and techniques are in **bold**

A

apricot shades, 77
Art Deco shades, 124
Aurora Borealis, 50–57
  Fancy Yarn, 57
  variation 1, 52
  variation 2, 53
  variation 3, 54, 56
  variation 4, 55, 56
autumnal shades, 98, 129

B

bag, shoulder, 117
Bargello Museum, Florence, 8, 110
bargello work, 8
Basket Weave, 76–83,152
  Fancy Yarn, 82
  lampshade, 83
  variation 1, 78
  variation 2, 79
  variation 3, 80
  variation 4, 81
berry shades, 112
black, use of, 59
blackberry shades, 111
Blazing Baubles, 148–149
blocking techniques, 13
blonde shades, 95
blue shades, 57, 60–61, 69, 94, 122, 143, 152–153
Bohemian shades, 85
bold tones, 119
Bollywood pattern, 47
Boxed Hungarian Point, 84–91
  Fancy Yarn, 90
  variation 1, 86
  variation 2, 87
  variation 3, 88
  variation 4, 89
  wall hanging, 91
burgundy shades, 63
Byzantine stitch, 36

C

canvas, 12–13
Chains (edging/border work), 134–135
champagne shades, 151
chocolate brown, use of, 87, 98
citrus shades, 53, 78
claret hues, 90
Climbing Brick Stitch, 16, 132, 138–139, 150, 152, 154
colour limits, 68
colour palette, 62
contrast, shades, 70
cool palette, 111
coral shades, 154–155
cream shades, 95, 116
Crossed Spiral Bands (edging/border work), 130–131
Curve Stitch, 18, 68, 128, 154
curves, 128–129
cushions, 9, 26, 65, 109, 125, 156

D

Diagonal Stripes (edging/border work), 132–133
diamond shapes, 148
DK acrylics/cottons, 11
Double Cross Stitch, 142–143
duo canvas, 12

E

eight-colour designs, 68, 110
English country garden shades, 111
evening tones, 49

F

Fancy Yarn
  Aurora Borealis, 57
  Basket Weave, 82
  Boxed Hungarian Point, 90
  Lanterns, 124
  Lollipops, 99
  Peaks, 64
  Zigzag, 43
feathered yarn, 82
fiery palette, 117
Flame, 44–49
  variation 1, 46
  variation 2, 47
  variation 3, 48
  variation 4, 49
Flame Stitch, 21, 44
Florentine stitch, 44
four-colour designs, 110, 113
foxy tones, 105
fruit shades
  bright, 79
  muted, 43, 79
fuchsia, bright, 52
funky shades, 141
Fused Spiral Bands (edging/border work), 136–137

G

geometric patterns, 58, 144–149
glittery yarn, 43, 82, 124
Gobelin filling stitch see **Climbing Brick Stitch**
gold shades, 49, 56–57, 60–61, 90, 116, 122, 151
grapefruit shades, 78
green shades, 52, 69, 98, 139

H

Hexagons, 146–147
Honeycombs, 154–155
hoops, 10
hues, 37, 90, 120
Hungarian Stitch, 22–23, 84, 118
hydrangea, shades of, 89

I

ice-blue palette, 108
ice-cream shades, 98
Inca shades, 135
Irish shades, 48

J

jewel shades, 103

L

lampshade, 83
Lanterns, 118–125
  cushion, 125
  Fancy Yarn, 124
  variation 1, 120
  variation 2, 121
  variation 3, 122
  variation 4, 123
lavender-blue shades, 86
lavender-green shades, 86
Leaf stitch, 20, 140–141
Lego effect, 81
lemon shades, 149
lime shades, 111
Lollipops, 152
Lollipops, 92–99
  Fancy Yarn, 99
  variation 1, 94
  variation 2, 95
  variation 3, 96, 98
  variation 4, 97, 98
Lozenges, 152–153
lurex yarns, 11

CREDITS

We would like to thank the following companies for generously supplying materials to make the bargello samples in this book:

SIRDAR
WEST YORKSHIRE
Est_1880

Sirdar Holdings Limited
Flanshaw Lane,
Wakefield, West Yorkshire
WF2 9ND UK

www.sirdar.com
Tel: 01924 371501
Order email: ORDERS@SIRDAR.CO.UK

Social media
Facebook: KnitSirdar
Instagram: @knitsirdar

ZWEIGART®
THE needlework fabric

Zweigart
www.zweigart.de